Collins

Japanese

Phrase Book & Dictionary

D0037216

Other languages in the *Collins Phrase Book & Dictionary* series:

FRENCH
GERMAN
GREEK
ITALIAN
PORTUGUESE
SPANISH

These titles are also published in a Language pack containing
60-minute CD/cassette and phrase book

Consultant: Sho Takahashi
Additional language consultant: Paul Callomon

HarperCollins*Publishers*
Westerhill Road,
Bishopbriggs, Glasgow G64 2QT

www.collins.co.uk

First published 2004

Reprint 10 9 8 7 6 5 4 3 2 1

© HarperCollins*Publishers* 2004

ISBN 0 00-716599-4

Typeset by Davidson Pre-Press Graphics Ltd, Glasgow

Printed in Italy by Amadeus SpA

Introduction

Your *Collins Phrase Book & Dictionary* is a handy, quick-reference guide that will help you make the most of your stay abroad. Its clear layout will save you valuable time when you need that crucial word or phrase. There are four main sections in this book:

Everyday Japan – photoguide

Packed full of photos, this section allows you to see all the practical visual information that will help with using ticket machines, driving on motorways, reading signs, etc.

Phrases

Practical topics are arranged thematically with an opening section Key talk containing vital phrases that should stand you in good stead in most situations.

Phrases are short, useful and each one has a pronunciation guide so that there is no problem saying them.

Eating out

This section contains phrases for ordering food and drink (and special requirements) plus a photoguide showing different eating places, menus and practical information to help choose the best options. A short menu reader helps identify favourite foods.

Dictionary

The practical English-Japanese (romaji) Dictionary means that you won't be stuck for words.

And finally, there is a short Grammar section explaining how the language works.

So, just flick through the pages to find the information you need. Why not start with a look at **Pronouncing Japanese** on page 6. From there on the going is easy with your *Collins Phrase Book & Dictionary*.

Useful websites

Information about Japan
www.cia.gov/cia/publications/
factbook/geos/ja.html
(*country profile of Japan*)
www.jnto.go.jp (*Japan
National Tourist Organization*)

Currency Converter
www.x-rates.com

Foreign Office Advice
www.fco.gov.uk/travel/
countryadvice.asp

Passport Office
www.ukpa.gov.uk

Health advice
www.thetraveldoctor.com
www.doh.gov.uk/traveladvice

Weather
www.bbc.co.uk/weather

Transport
www.jnto.go.jp/eng/GA/
(*information on getting
around Japan*)
www.japanrailpass.net
(*information on Japan Rail
Pass*)
www.narita-airport.or.jp/
(*information on Narita
International airport*)

Driving
www.jaf.or.jp/e/index_e.htm
(*Japan Automobile
Federation – JAF*)

Sightseeing
www.jnto.go.jp (*Japan
National Tourist Organization*)
www.japan-guide.com (*guide
to Japan*)
www.hatobus.co.jp/english/
index.html (*coach sightseeing
tours of Tokyo*)
www.pref.nara.jp (*website to
Nara prefecture*)

Internet Cafés
www.cybercafes.com

Outdoor Activities
www.outdoorjapan.com
(*information about hiking,
onsen – hot springs, camping,
golf, etc*)

Hotels & Accommodation
www.abouthotel.com
www.jnto.go.jp (*this site has
accommodation*)

Food
www.bento.com (*a guide to
Japanese cuisine and eating
out in Tokyo*)

Contents

Pronouncing Japanese

Although Japanese has an extremely complicated writing system, it is a grammatically simple language that is very easy to pronounce. Provided you follow a few set rules and learn a few set phrases, you will be surprised at how far you can get by.

The basic unit of speech is the syllable, not the letter. Every syllable is pronounced quite evenly and rather flatly, and stress is much more subtle. For example, Paris is pronounced **PAris** in English and **paREE** in French, while in Japanese it is **PA-REE** – with equal stress on both syllables.

Japanese has relatively few sounds. Vowels have only one sound (rather like Italian):

Vowels

a is pronounced as in *bath*

e is pronounced as in *let*

i is pronounced as in *police*

o is pronounced as in *got*

u is pronounced as in *put*

Vowel combinations

Japanese vowels differ from English ones in that they do not change their sounds when combined with other vowels. To pronounce the kai of kaizen, for example, you simply say ka (as in 'cart') and i (as in 'bit') without a pause.

ai is pronounced as in Th*ai*land

ae is pronounced as if it were hyphenated *a-eh*

ei is pronounced as in n*eigh*

A bar on top of a vowel indicates that it is twice as long, e.g. in the case of **Kyōto** the first *o* is double the length of the second one. You should take care to pronounce these long vowels clearly otherwise the meaning of the word may change.

Consonants (*b*, *c*, *s*, *t*, etc) are close to their English equivalents, but note the following:

g is always hard, as in *golf*, never as in *Germany*

y is always pronounced as in *young*, never as in *cry*

Double consonants, like the double 't' in *kitte*, are pronounced by leaving a very slight pause before the consonant, then expressing it very clearly, as if the word had two halves. For example: *kite* has the same stress as the English 'kitty', but *kitte* sounds more like 'kids' day'.

Since Japanese lacks the consonants *l* and *v*, foreign loanwords with these letters are pronounced with *r* and *b*, respectively. Thus, the three English words 'love', 'lab' and 'rub', all become indistinguishable as *ra-bu* in Japanese.

Japanese also lacks the *si* sound (as in 'to sit'), and *shi* is used instead, with often embarrassing results, e.g. 'babysitter' becomes *be-bi-shi-ttā*! Other English sounds that do not exist in Japanese are *hu* (as in 'hook'; *fu* is used instead), *th* (as in 'thin'; *sh* is used instead) and *ti* (as in 'tin'; *chi* is used instead).

Remember to pronounce each syllable clearly and separately. Foreign loanwords (including your own name) are 'Japanized' by making each syllable end in a vowel. Thus, Mr Smith becomes *Mi-su-tā Su-mi-su*, Grand Hotel becomes *Gu-ra-n-do Ho-te-ru* and taxi becomes *ta-ku-shī*. However u and i are pronounced very faintly, so *Mi-su-tā* becomes *mista* and *gu-ra-n-do* becomes *grando*. The only exception is when a word ends with the letter *n*, like *supāman* 'Superman'. If you don't know the Japanese for a word, Japanizing the English equivalent may well work.

You should also remember that Japanese does not have a silent *e* at the end of a word such as in the English 'to take'. If 'take' is read as the Japanese word *take* (bamboo), it should be pronounced *tah-keh*. Similarly with *sake* (rice wine), pronounced *sah-keh*, or *ike* (pond), pronounced *eeh-keh*, etc.

Map of Japan

HOKKAIDŌ

Sapporo

JAPAN SEA

Morioka

Sendai

Nigata

HONSHŪ

Tōkyō

Mt. Fuji

Nagoya

Kyōto

Kōbe

Hiroshima

Ōsaka

Fukuoka

SHIKOKU

KYŪSHŪ

Nagasaki

PACIFIC OCEAN

何時来ても　もうと便利に！

24 時間

OPEN 24 HOURS

Shops open from 10am to 8pm, seven days a week (including public holidays, except for New Year).

開 **OPEN**

閉 **CLOSED**

非常口 EXIT

EMERGENCY EXIT
As well as Japanese writing, you see pictograms used.

PARKING ENTRANCE

P 入口

Entrance

Japanese script is based on Chinese-derived characters called *kanji*.

出口 **EXIT**

入 **IN**　出 **OUT**

JAPANESE WRITING

 C 城建古墳の墳丘には屋中（りゅう）天皇陵古墳がある。

古事記、日本書紀によると、都十代の崇神天皇は、奈良盆地の東の三輪山を神の山として、その麓に拠点を置いて国を治めたという。おそらくこれが大和政権の起源であり、三世紀末から西世紀初の初めの頃と考えられる。以後、この地を開店とした

Japanese can be written in two ways, either horizontally or vertically. The more traditional way is from top to bottom, starting at the right-hand top corner of the page. With modernization, it also became written horizontally from left to right.

9

Everyday Japan

2 litres

symbol for yen

Prices are generally written with western numbers as are weights and time. Japan is fully metric.

Symbol for yen. It is pronounced **en** not yen. The international symbol is ¥.

5,000円

Thousands of yen are separated by a comma. Once it reaches millions, the numbers are separated by a full stop. Japan is still largely a cash society – get used to carrying large wads of banknotes.

MONEY

Coins are ¥1 (aluminium), ¥5 (brass with hole in middle), ¥10 (brass), ¥50 (nickel with hole in middle), ¥100 and ¥500. All coins except ¥5 have western numerals on them. Notes are ¥1,000, ¥2,000, ¥5,000 and ¥10,000

logo for post office

Most ATMs in Japan do not accept cards of non-Japanese banks. Many only work during banking hours, so it would not be wise to rely on obtaining cash from them.

logo for post office cash machine

BANK HOURS
Banks are open 9am – 3pm, Mon-Fri and closed at weekends and on public holidays.

Citibank, which has branches in all the big cities, is most orientated to dealing with foreigners.

You can change money easily at Narita Airport.

There are automatic paying machines for tickets, parking, etc. You can use cash and the major international credit cards.

A 5% consumption tax (equivalent to VAT) is added to prices (except for a number of everyday items such as stamps and newspapers). So for a 1000-yen item you will be asked to pay 1005 yen. To avoid breaking into another note, have a pocketful of small change to pay the tax.

There is no tipping in Japan – in restaurants there is a service charge (usually 10%) plus the consumption charge.

11

Japan has a population of approximately 127 million and cities can become awfully crowded – especially on public transport during the rush hour or at shopping centres at weekends.

Space is a premium in Japan and high prices charged in some places (like traditional coffee shops) reflect this. The high charge isn't so much for the drink but for the space rented out. You can stay for as long as you like.

Traditional Japanese buildings were made of wood. The more traditional an eating or drinking establishment, the more often wood is used in its decor.

UMBRELLA STANDS

During the rainy season, you will need an umbrella for the frequent showers.

Streets are kept immaculately clean. There is no litter and there are recycling bins outside shops.

NO SMOKING

Smoking is still very popular in Japan – bars, in particular, can become very smoky.

KARAOKE

Karaoke booths are extremely popular and you find that time can become distorted in them. What feels like an hour to you is probably more likely to be five hours!

If you are invited to do a turn at the microphone, forget any inhibitions and enjoy yourself.

TO LET

Phone numbers are written in western numerals.

FOOD DISPLAY

Many eating establishments have a display of plates with plastic food on them to show you what they offer.

Everyday Japan

WATER
Tap water is safe to drink all over Japan. However in the hot, muggy summer, it is worth carrying a small bottle of mineral water around with you.

VENDING MACHINES
Jidohanbaki (shortened to *jihanki*) is the word for vending machine. You can get practically anything from them: hot tea and coffee in a tin, cold tea, cold beer, tights, knickers, etc. Hot drinks will be identified with red buttons, cold with blue. Ones selling alcohol shut down at night.

PUSH   **PULL**

READING JAPANESE

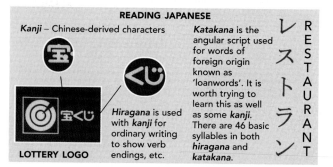

Kanji – Chinese-derived characters

LOTTERY LOGO

Hiragana is used with *kanji* for ordinary writing to show verb endings, etc.

Katakana is the angular script used for words of foreign origin known as 'loanwords'. It is worth trying to learn this as well as some *kanji*. There are 46 basic syllables in both *hiragana* and *katakana*.

レストラン
RESTAURANT

Everyday Japan

SIGNS TO LOCAL PLACES
In big cities, signs will be in Japanese and English. Outside of the main cities they will just be in Japanese.

PEDESTRIAN AREA
Many signs are internationally recognizable.

FIRE HYDRANT

Many signs are located high above the street.

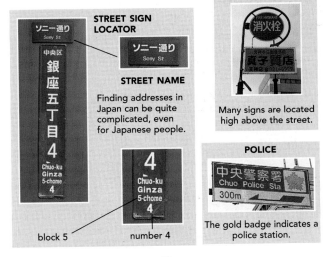

STREET SIGN LOCATOR

STREET NAME

Finding addresses in Japan can be quite complicated, even for Japanese people.

block 5

number 4

POLICE

The gold badge indicates a police station.

Many streets in Japanese cities are narrow and more suitable to bicycles, motorbikes and small cars. Although city centres are congested with cars, private ownership is not as common in Japan because of the cost. You have to pay for parking space, it doesn't automatically come with your dwelling. Toll roads are also very expensive.

Outside main cities there is not a great deal of traffic.

BICYCLES

Bikes are used routinely in Japan. There are bike lanes on pavements which you should look out for.

DO NOT ABANDON BIKE SIGN

BIKE PARKING

There is ample parking for bikes in Japanese cities. Many bikes have footrests on the back for a passenger to stand on. You can hire bikes from youth hostels and cycling terminals.

PARKING
There is no roadside parking in cities except in designated areas. There are car parks, parking meters and multistorey car parks.

Time remaining.

SPACES
Look out for red script if the car park is full.

Space-saving Japanese parking.

DRIVING
Driving is on the left and speeds are in kilometres per hour.

No overtaking – 50kph speed limit.

Care should be taken on windy roads, some Japanese drivers tend to cut corners and you should use your car horn on approaching sharp bends.

GIVE WAY

PETROL
Petrol stations are not self-service. A number of personnel will come out to tend to your needs. The word 'gasoline' is more widely understood than 'petrol'.

Timetables

DAYS

月曜	**Monday** *getsu-yōbi*
火曜	**Tuesday** *ka-yōbi*
水曜	**Wednesday** *sui-yōbi*
木曜	**Thursday** *moku-yōbi*
金曜	**Friday** *kin-yōbi*
土曜	**Saturday** *do-yōbi*
日曜	**Sunday** *nichi-yōbi*

MONTHS

一月	**January** *ichi-gats*
二月	**February** *ni-gats*
三月	**March** *san-gats*
四月	**April** *shi-gats*
五月	**May** *go-gats*
六月	**June** *roku-gats*
七月	**July** *shichi-gats*
八月	**August** *hachi-gats*
九月	**September** *ku-gats*
十月	**October** *jū-gats*
十一月	**November** *jū-ichi-gats*
十二月	**December** *jū-ni-gats*

DATES

You see western numbers mixed with *kanji*. Dates are written with the year first, then the month and then the day.

24時まで営業

24-HOUR OPENING

18

READING TIMETABLES

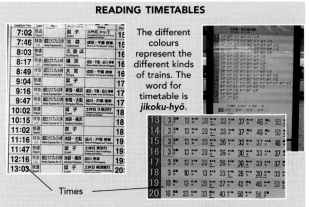

The different colours represent the different kinds of trains. The word for timetable is *jikoku-hyō*.

Times

DEPARTURES

FERRY TIMETABLE
Notice that the times on this ferry timetable are written in Japanese rather than western numerals. They are also written vertically. The further you go off the beaten track, the less westernization you find.

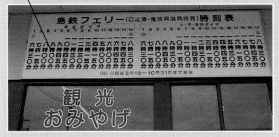

Getting around

JAPAN NATIONAL TOURIST ORGANIZATION

The JNTO website is full of practical information and useful links. You should visit it before your trip to Japan – *www.jnto.go.jp*. There are many TIC offices all over Japan. They provide maps and brochures in English.

TOURIST INFORMATION CENTER (TIC)

右 **RIGHT**   左 **LEFT**

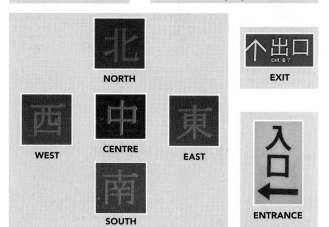

北 **NORTH**

西 **WEST**   中 **CENTRE**   東 **EAST**

南 **SOUTH**

出口 **EXIT**

入口 **ENTRANCE**

Getting around

BUS & TAXI STOP GUIDE

Japanese taxis are safe, metered and clean – but expensive.

There is no need to tip.

Taxis are more often to be found late at night outside main hotels.

Heavy traffic in cities means that the subway or trains are often better options.

TAXI STANCE
You can find taxi stances at stations and hotels. They can also be hailed in the street (provided the red light is illuminated).

The driver automatically opens the doors and boot, so stand well back.

There's a surcharge between 11pm and 5am.

BUS
When you board this type of bus you get a ticket with a number. As the bus continues along its route, the fareboard changes. You pay the appropriate fee at your destination for your number ticket.

Have someone write down your destination so that you can recognize it on the board.

Getting around

ENTRANCE TO SUBWAY
The underground system in Japan is known as the subway. Most lines link with the Japanese overground network.

銀座線
Ginza Line

The different lines are colour-coded.

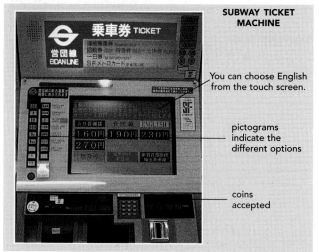

SUBWAY TICKET MACHINE

You can choose English from the touch screen.

pictograms
indicate the
different options

coins
accepted

Subway lines are colour-coded. The subway is the quickest, easiest and cheapest way of getting around large cities. Avoid the rush hours if you can.

SUBWAY ENTRANCES & EXITS

The different subway exits are numbered and marked on the map with English translations beneath.
Some stations have many levels and exits. The word for platform sounds like 'home'.

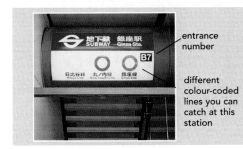

entrance number

different colour-coded lines you can catch at this station

Getting around

JAPANESE RAILWAY

logo for Japanese Railway (JR)

You can exchange the Japan Rail Pass voucher at the JR office at Narita Airport and use it on the Narita Express into Tokyo city centre.

The Japan Rail Pass has to be purchased before you arrive in Japan. Visit *www.japanrailpass.net* for details.

STATION KIOSK
You can get all the usual things: food, drink, books, gifts and travel goods.

OVERHEAD PLATFORM BOARD

Abbreviation for station.

platform number

The red line shows the next train and destination. The green line shows the train after it from this platform.

BULLET TRAIN — SHINKANSEN

Japanese trains are famous for sticking to timetables. Even a 10-minute delay is practically unheard of. Trains stop for a short time to let people on or off, so you have to move smartly.

RAILWAY STATIONS

Pictograms show all the facilities available.

The lower the number, the faster the service. Number 1 is the fastest train.

LUGGAGE LOCKER

Coin-operated luggage lockers tend to be quite small. Even on the trains, space for luggage is quite restricted. Travel as light as you can.

Colours correspond to the different types of trains.

Shopping

Most eating places have a board showing photos of the meals they offer.

Streets can get very crowded, especially at weekends. Try and choose a quiet time to shop.

All the branded chains can be found in the cities.

Tokyo is a good place to buy trainers as the fashion cycle is so fast that the major brands promote a vast array of styles and colours not found elsewhere (often with 50% discount).

PHOTOBOOTH
You have to carry personal identification (passport, identity card) with you at all times.

CONVENIENCE STORE
Most areas have a convenience store (*conbeni*) open 24 hours selling all manner of necessities. You can also buy a snack (pot noodle) which you can microwave there.

BOOKSHOP

24時まで営業 — 24-hour opening

Most shopping malls have a variety of eating places. The types of places are usually displayed photographically. The letter F stands for floor.

LIQUOR STORE

You have to be over twenty to buy alcohol in Japan. And over twenty to smoke.

PHARMACY

The green cross sign is used in Japan. Remember that Japanese people are usually slighter than westerners and you may require a slightly higher dose of medicine.

SHOE SHOP

Imported shoes are expensive in Japan because of the import tax. However, Japanese-made shoes are good value. Shoes are very popular with Japanese people.

Take some high fibre food bars with you to avoid constipation!

Shopping

MILK

Milk is called *miruku* or *gyūnyū*. Semi-skimmed milk is *teishibō gyūnyū*, skimmed milk is *mushibō gyūnyū*. Soya milk is *tōnyū*. When you order tea or coffee in a cafe you are generally given a small jug of milk.

BOTTLED WATER

Tap water in Japan is fine to drink, but many people prefer mineral water. It is also better for making some types of tea. Sparkling water is not as common as still water.

TODAY'S SPECIAL OFFER!

SASHIMI DISPLAY

Sashimi is raw fish. It is usually eaten on special occasions. The largest size would be for a family of 3 or 4. This is a dish that would not generally be prepared at home.

BREAD

The word for bread is *pan*.

FRUIT & VEGETABLES

In supermarkets nearly everything is shrinkwrapped and you need only choose what you want and take it to the checkout.

FISH DISPLAY

Fish is sold by the weight. The assistant cuts and weighs what you require. They also clean and gut it if you ask.

CHECKOUT

Checkouts operate as at home. They provide free plastic bags.

Many supermarkets operate a loyalty-card system and you may be asked if you have one.

Outside cities shops may not have a facility for taking credit cards.

Somewhere to stay

RYOKAN

Staying in a traditional Japanese inn (*ryokan*) allows you to experience Japanese traditional ways. The price usually includes dinner and breakfast. A *minshuku* is a cheaper version of the *ryokan*, usually bigger and only in main tourist resorts.

A maid arranges your bath, serves dinner in your room and lays out the futon for you to sleep on.

Ryokan provide towels, toiletries and nightwear in the form of a *yukata* (see right) – a cotton gown that can be worn indoors and should be worn in the hotel once you are checked in. Both men and women wear them.

You are served your meals in your room. Take care not to wear shoes on the *tatami* matting.

HOTEL RATES

Japan offers a wide range of accommodation.

CAPSULE HOTEL

These hotels comprise tiny self-contained cubicles stacked on top of each other, with communal washing facilities and vending machines for food, drink and toiletries.

LOVE HOTEL

'Love hotels' are not as sleazy as they sound – they are often luxurious, clean and rooms often have great decor.

They offer couples total discretion and privacy for 2-hour periods during the day. They're also used by Japanese married couples to get some privacy.

Overnight stays (generally after 10pm and checking out before 10am) get cheaper rates.

Toilets & baths

Standard pictograms are used to indicate men's, ladies' and disabled toilets.

DISABLED TOILET
Sign showing opening hours.

TOILETS

There is a great deal of delicacy associated with using the toilet. On trains there are western-style sit-on toilets and Japanese crouch over toilets (see below). Elsewhere mostly western predominate. In a public toilet there is no hand towel or blow-dryer. You need to carry a little face cloth with you. If you need to buy one they are called *o-tefuki* and you can buy them easily (even branded ones such as Calvin Klein or Burberry!).

The bathroom and toilet are always kept separate, and you will find a pair of toilet slippers to use, leaving your own outside the door. Never leave smells in the toilet in a private house. There will usually be a deodorant spray to use. There may be a little box on the wall. This is not an alarm, it makes the noise of flushing to give you extra privacy.

Check before using the toilet that you can see the toilet handle. If there is none, crouch in front and feel over the body of the toilet. You will find a little secret drawer, like on a CD player. Before you test all the buttons, stand back in case you get sprayed by the bidet function!

button to make flushing noise.

To use a Japanese-style toilet, you squat and face the 'windscreen' end. Check you can squat and make sure you don't have loose change in your back pocket!

TOILETS

Western-style toilets are very advanced with warm seats and wash and blow-dry options. Most flats are not centrally heated so the warm seat can be very nice in winter. A warmed-seat toilet is called a *Warmlet*. The *Washlet* has a button called Bidet which does a front wash. The *Derriere* button does a back wash. There will also be a button for drying.

TISSUE VENDING MACHINE

Always carry tissues with you as they are often not available in public toilets.

JAPANESE BATH

You must shower three times at the shower stool before entering a traditional Japanese bath (or *onsen* – hot spring, or *sento* – public bath). *Onsen* and *sento* have large shared pools so you need to be clean before entering. There will be a changing room where you put your clothes into a basket and wrap a cotton towel around you. Take a larger towel with you for drying (or hire one at the desk). The wash

area has individual tap, bowls and stool areas. You soap and rinse all over, pouring or scooping the water from the bowl. Then make sure that you empty your bowl and sluice it down along with the shower utensils and stool before entering the bath or hot spring. On no account take soap into the *onsen* or *sento*. You need to be squeaky clean before entering it.

Japanese life

Always remove shoes when entering someone's home or before sitting on tatami matting.

ONSEN

You should try and visit a hot spring during your visit. The website *www.outdoor.japan.com/onsen/onsen -introduction.html/* has details and information. If you are a westerner and sharing with Japanese folk, be prepared to feel like a giant. Watching the sunset from an outdoor pool is a must.

Most Japanese homes have a shrine in the living room. It may just be a simple raised platform with a vase or wall hanging (see above).

Japan has 2 major religions – *shintō* and buddhism. This characteristic gate called *tori* is one of the many shrines you can visit.

The old parts of Japan were built in wood. This means that much of it has been lost to fire.

Summer in Japan can be very humid with frequent showers. The cherry blossom is out from early to late April (earlier, the further south you are). Autumn is when the maple leaves turn crimson and the days are clear and cool. Major national holidays are Golden week (late April/early May) and *Obon* (mid-August).

Some Japanese homes have an outdoor shrine (see above). These are looked after and even decorated with clothing. The boxes on the right contain branches from the tree which Japanese people take to the cemeteries.

POST OFFICE LOGO
Post offices are open from 9am–5pm Mon–Fri and closed at weekends.

Postboxes are red. If there are 2 slits, one is for local mail, the other for elsewhere. Collection times are indicated.

Letters can be addressed in romaji (western letters) but write clearly and in capitals. Here it is written from right to left and from top to bottom. The city is written first and the addressee last. The small printed boxes on envelopes and postcards are for the post or zip code (*yūbin bangō*).

You can get phonecards for domestic and international use. Green-coloured phones take coins and cards. You can make international calls from green and gold ones.

different cards available

Phone numbers are written in western numerals. 0120 is a freephone number.

INTERNATIONAL DIALLING CODES	
JAPAN	00 81
US/CANADA	00 1
UK	00 44
AUSTRALIA	00 61

You can hire mobile phones at Narita and Kansai Airports. Your own phone won't work in Japan.

The word for 'at' is *atto*.

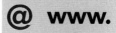

www dot is said as in English.

- English is learnt at school in Japan, but mostly reading and translating, not so much speaking.
- There are levels of politeness in Japanese and although it would be impossible for a foreigner to be aware of them all, care should be taken to act politely and not be too loud.
- *Sumimasen* is an all-purpose word. You can use it to attract someone's attention before making a request. You can use it in a crowded train to get past people. It also means 'sorry'!

hello/good afternoon	**goodbye**	**bye**
kon-nichi wa	sayonara	bai-bai
こんにちわ	さようなら	バイバイ

good morning	**good evening**	**good night**
ohayō gozaimass	konban wa	oyasumi nasai
おはようございます	こんばんわ	おやすみなさい

good morning Mrs Nakamura *(polite)*
Nakamura-san, ohayō gozaimass
中村さん、おはようございます

please	**thank you**	**thanks very much**
dōzo	arigatō	dōmo arigatō
どうぞ	ありがとう	どうもありがとう

yes	**no**
hai	ī-e
はい	いいえ

yes please	**no thank you**
hai onegai shimass	kekkō dess
はいお願いします	結構です

excuse me!/sorry!	**I'm very sorry**
sumimasen	mōshiwake arimasen
すみません	申し訳ありません

Key Talk

● US English is more widely understood in Japan. Remember to use 'subway' rather than underground and 'gasoline' rather than petrol, if you find you are not being understood.
● Even if you don't know the Japanese word for something, try Japanizing the English word and adding **kudasai** (please).
● Japanese is based on syllables so card = **kādo**, beer = **bīru**, tour = **tsuā** (see **Pronouncing Japanese**, p6).

Mr ... / Mrs ... / Ms ...
...-san
...さん

are you Mrs Nakamura?
Nakamura-san dess ka?
中村さんですか？

my name is Caroline Smart
watashi wa Caroline Smart dess
私はキャロライン　スマートです

do you understand?
wakarimass ka?
わかりますか？

I don't understand
wakarimasen
わかりません

do you speak English?
eigo o hanasemass ka?
英語を話せますか？

I don't speak Japanese
watashi wa nihongo o hanasemasen
私は日本語を話せません

excuse me
sumimasen
すみません

please help me
tetsudatte kudasai
手伝ってください

what is this?
kore wa nan dess ka?
これはなんですか？

this one please
kore o kudasai
これを下さい

that one please
sore o kudasai
それを下さい

● Japanese tend not to use assertive words like 'yes' and 'no'.
A good alternative for 'yes' is ī dess ne, meaning 'that's lovely'.
● ī-e (meaning 'no') is best avoided. Looking doubtful works
well and a good alternative to use is **gomen nasai,** meaning
'I am sorry'.
● If a Japanese is saying 'no', they are more likely to let their
reply tail off and not finish the sentence. This conveys 'no' by
indicating that there is some difficulty with what you have asked.

... please
... o kudasai
... を下さい

a coffee please
kōhī o kudasai
コーヒーを下さい

a coca cola please
koka-kora o kudasai
コカコーラを下さい

I would like .../please can I have ...
... onegai shimass
... お願いします

I would like a glass
gurass onegai shimass
グラスお願いします

I would like a fork
fōku onegai shimass
フォークお願いします

do you have ...?
... wa arimass ka?
... はありますか？

do you have a map?
chizu wa arimass ka?
地図はありますか？

do you have stamps?
kitte ga arimass ka?
切手はありますか？

do you have postcards?
postokādo wa arimass ka?
ポストカードはありますか？

do you have milk?
miruku wa arimass ka?
牛乳はありますか？

Key Talk

0120-b
平日 8:30~18:00 土・日
空港宅配料金 (通常料金)

- Japanese people who speak English are likely to come up to a foreigner and offer help if they see them looking lost.
- Have cards made with your name and address. They don't need to be elaborate – ones you print yourself and cut up are fine.
- When you receive a business card, examine it carefully and try to pronounce the name. Then make sure you are seen putting it carefully into your wallet.

how much is/are …?
… wa ikura dess ka?
… はいくらですか？

how much is that?
sore wa ikura dess ka?
それはいくらですか？

how much are the bananas?
banana wa ikura dess ka?
バナナはいくらですか？

how much is the map?
chizu wa ikura dess ka?
地図はいくらですか？

how much is the camera?
kamera wa ikura dess ka?
カメラはいくらですか？

how much is the entrance fee?
nyū-jō-ryō wa ikura dess ka?
入場料はいくらですか？

where is/are …?
… wa doko dess ka?
… はどこですか？

where is the bank?
ginkō wa doko dess ka?
銀行はどこですか？

where is the tourist office?
ryokō annai-jo wa doko dess ka?
旅行案内所はどこですか？

where is the toilet?
toire wa doko dess ka?
トイレはどこですか？

where is the hotel?
hoteru wa doko dess ka?
ホテルはどこですか？

the nearest …
ichiban chikai …
一番近い …

where is the nearest …?
ichiban chikai … wa doko dess ka?
一番近い　はどこですか？

● *You should address someone you meet by their surname followed by **-san** (for both men and women). So Mrs Junko Hara would be **Hara-san** to most people she knows. If you get on very well, she will ask you to call her Junko and you would call her **Junko-san**. If you miss off the **-san** or use the first name without express permission, you will cause shock!*

● *You're more likely to be addressed by your first name followed by **-san**, e.g. **Carol-san**, because this is how you are generally known.*

where is the nearest pharmacy?
ichiban chikai yakkyok wa doko dess ka?
一番近い薬局はどこですか？

where is the nearest hotel?
ichiban chikai hoteru wa doko dess ka?
一番近いホテルはどこですか？

where is the nearest police box?
ichiban chikai kōban wa doko dess ka?
一番近い交番はどこですか？

is it ...?	**is it far?**	**is it nearby?**
... dess ka?	tōi dess ka?	chikai dess ka?
ですか？	遠いですか？	近いですか？

is/are there ...?
... wa arimass ka?
... はありますか？

is there a ryokan?
ryokan wa arimass ka?
旅館はありますか？

is there a hot spring?
onsen wa arimass ka?
温泉はありますか？

there is/are no ...
... wa arimasen
... はありません

there are no towels
taoru wa arimasen
タオルはありません

Key Talk

● *You shouldn't eat or drink while walking along the street or on public transport. You will find the streets very clean and there are numerous recycling bins outside shops.*

● *Japan is a very safe country and there is very little chance of being robbed or mugged.*

● *Guests are normally entertained in restaurants. If you are a business visitor, you will be taken out and not invited to a home. However, a tourist might be invited to a Japanese home.*

I need …
… o onegai shimass
… をお願いします

I need a receipt
reshīto o onegai shimass
レシートをお願いします

I need to phone
denwa o kaketai dess
電話をかけたいです

I need a taxi
takshī o yonde kudasai
タクシーを呼んでください

may I/we …?
… shtemo ī dess ka?
…してもいいですか？

may I drive?
unten shtemo ī dess ka?
運転してもいいですか？

where can I buy a camera?
kamera wa doko de kaemass ka?
カメラはどこで買えますか？

where can I buy a mobile phone?
keitai denwa wa doko de kaemass ka?
携帯電話はどこで買えますか？

how do I work this?
dono yō ni tsukaeba i dess ka?
どのように使えばいいですか？

what's this called in Japanese?
kore wa nihongo de nan to īmass ka?
これは日本語で何と言いますか？

Key Talk

- *Always make sure you have no holes in your socks/tights, as you may have to take off your shoes unexpectedly.*
- *Always remove shoes when entering someone's home or before stepping onto **tatami** matting. Some Japanese restaurants have **tatami** matting and you will have to remove your shoes.*
- *Summers are very humid in most of Japan, so carry some water, a small towel and a fan with you.*

when?
itsu?
いつ？

at what time?
nan-ji ni?
何時に？

when does the train leave?
densha wa nan-ji ni demass ka?
電車は何時に出ますか？

when is check-out time?
chekk-auto wa nan-ji dess ka?
チェックアウトは何時ですか？

when do you open?
itsu akimass ka?
いつ開きますか？

when do you close?
itsu shimarimass ka?
いつ閉まりますか？

this morning
kesa
今朝

this afternoon
gogo
午後

this evening
konya
今夜

today
kyō
今日

tomorrow
ashta
明日

yesterday
kinō
昨日

now
ima
今

later
ato de
あとで

Key Talk

● *Personal space is important to Japanese people – don't sit or stand too close to them when talking.*
● *You should speak softly. Japanese don't like loud voices.*
● *When blowing your nose in public, be as quiet and unobtrusive as possible. Use paper tissues, as Japanese use handkerchiefs to wipe hands and foreheads.*
● *You shouldn't point at people with your index finger – use your whole hand, palm upwards in a flowing motion.*

I'm …
watashi wa … dess
私は … です

British/Australian/American
igiriss-jin/ōstoraria-jin/amerika-jin
イギリス人/オーストラリア人/アメリカ人

my name is Jane Shaw
watashi wa jane shaw dess
私はジェーン ショウです

what is your name?
o-namae wa nan dess ka?
お名前は何ですか？

how are you?
o-genki dess ka?
お元気ですか？

fine thanks, and you?
genki dess, anata wa?
元気です，あなたは？

I'm here on holiday
kyūka de koko ni imass
休暇でここにいます

I'm here on business
shigoto de koko ni imass
仕事でここにいます

this is my first trip to Japan
nihon wa hajimete dess
日本は初めてです

this is my first trip to Tokyo
tōkyō wa hajimete dess
東京は初めてです

Key Talk

- Gift-exchanging is very important in Japan and there are a few useful points to remember.
- If you are invited to someone's home, remember to take a gift, preferably something from your own country. Take care to wrap it as prettily as possible, even if it isn't expensive. Take more gifts than you think you could possibly need!
- When you receive a gift, you should show how delighted you are and even ask for a photo to be taken of you, your hosts and the gift.

have you ever been abroad?
gaikok ni itta koto ga arimass ka?
外国にいった事がありますか？

I enjoyed that very much
taihen tanoshikatta dess
大変楽しかったです

that was a feast!
go-chisō-sama deshta
ごちそうさまでした

thank you so much
arigatō gozaimass
ありがとうございます

that was very kind of you, many thanks
o-sewa ni narimashta, arigatō gozaimashta
お世話になりました。ありがとうございます

I'm going out
itte kimass
いってきます

(reply to this)
itte rasshai
いってらっしゃい

it was very nice to meet you
o-ai dekite tanoshikatta dess
お会いできて楽しかったです

this is my address
watashi no jūsho dess
私の住所です

this is my phone number
wastashi no denwa-bango dess
私の電話番号です

Money – changing

● Japan is still largely a cash society. You get used to carrying around wads of banknotes, especially outside the big cities where it is more difficult to get cash.
● Banks are open 9am–3pm Mon–Fri and closed Saturdays, Sundays and on public holidays.
● Foreign currency can be changed only at banks with the sign 'Authorized Foreign Exchange Bank' and Post Offices. Citibank is the most orientated to dealing with foreigners.

where is the nearest bank?
ichiban chikai ginkō wa doko dess ka?
一番近い銀行はどこですか？

where is the nearest bureau de change?
ichiban chikai ryōgae-jo wa doko dess ka?
一番近い両替所はどこですか？

where is the cash machine?
ginkō no ATM wa doko dess ka?
銀行のATMはどこですか？

please show me
misete kudasai
見せてください

I would like to change … into yen
… o en ni kaetai dess
… を円に換えて下さい

British pounds
igiriss pondo
イギリスポンド

US	**Australian**	**dollars**
amerika	ōstoraria	doru
アメリカ	オーストラリア	ドル

what is the rate for …?
… rēto wa ikura dess ka?
… レートはいくらですか？

please change this
kore o kaete kudasai
これを替えて下さい

can I get cash with this credit card?
kono krejitto kādo de genkin o hiki-dasemass ka?
このクレジットカードで現金を引き出せますか？

spending – Money

- *Credit cards are only accepted in the more expensive hotels, shops and restaurants.*
- *Cash machines (ATM) are widespread but many don't accept cards of non-Japanese banks. Service is often restricted to banking hours.*
- *If you plan to travel outside main cities, take wads of cash.*
- *A 5% consumption tax is added to prices (except for tickets, newspapers and stamps) afterwards. So for a 100-yen item, you pay 105 yen.*

the bill please
o-kanjō onegai shimass
お勘定お願いします

how much is it?
ikura dess ka?
いくらですか？

do I pay in advance?
maebarai dess ka?
前払いできますか？

where do I pay?
doko de haraeba ī dess ka?
どこで払えばいいですか？

can I pay with this credit card?
kono krejitto-kādo de haraemass ka?
このクレジットカードで払えますか？

can I pay with these traveller's cheques?
kono toraberāzu chekk de haraemass ka?
このトラベルチェックで払えますか？

please give me a receipt
reshīto o onegai shimass
レシートをお願いします

please give me an itemized bill
meisai o onegai shimass
明細をおねがいします

I will pay for this
watashi ga haraimass
私が払います

this is on me!
watashi no ogori dess!
私のおごりです

Airport

- Most signs will be in Japanese and English.
- Most people working at the airport will understand and speak some English.
- There are tourist information centres at the main airports.
- Visit www.narita-airport.or.jp for info.
- You can exchange your Japan Rail voucher at Narita International airport and use the Japan Rail Pass on the Narita Express into Tokyo.

to the airport please
kūkō made onegai shimass
空港までお願いします

how do I get into town?
machi made dōyatte ikeba ī dess ka?
街までどうやって行けばいいですか？

where is the information desk?
annai-jo wa doko dess ka?
案内所はどこですか？

where is the JR ticket information office?
JR no ryokō mado-guchi wa doko dess ka?
JRの案内所はどこですか？

where is the train to ...?
...-yuki no densha wa doko dess ka?
... 行きの電車はどこですか？

where is the bus to ...?
...-yuki no bass wa doko dess ka?
... 行きのバスはどこですか？

where is the check-in desk for ...?
... no chekk-in kauntā wa doko dess ka?
... のチェックインカウンターはどこですか？

Customs & Passports

- UK, US, Canadian and Australian visitors to Japan do not require a visa for short business trips and holidays.
- Visit **www.narita-airport-customs.go.jp** to find out about allowances.
- Japanese law requires you to carry proof of identity at all times, so make sure that you always carry your passport.
- Innoculations aren't required unless arriving from an infected area.
- Drug penalties in Japan are extremely high.

my passport
watashi no passpōto
私のパスポート

my visa
watashi no biza
私のビザ

I have ... nationality
... kokseki dess
... 国籍です

British/Australian/US
igiriss/ōstoraria/amerika
イギリス/オーストラリア/アメリカ

I came here on holiday
kyūka de koko ni kimashta
休暇でここにきました

I came here on business
shigoto de koko ni kimashta
仕事でここにきました

I have nothing to declare
shinkok suru mono wa arimasen
申告する物はありません

the children are on this passport
kodomotachi mo kono passpōto
子供たちもこのパスポートです

it's a present
prezento dess
プレゼントです

it's for my personal use
watashi ga tsukau mono dess
私が使う物です

Asking the Way – questions

日比谷公会堂
Hibiya Public Hall
日比谷図書館
Hibiya Library

- When asking directions in public, approach younger people if possible. Older people are likely to become flustered if addressed by a foreigner.
- Almost all street names are written in Japanese script only.
- Before you go anywhere, ask a Japanese person to write down the address, the nearest station or bus stop, the phone number and name of your host and draw a small map in Japanese. You can then ask for directions if you get lost.

excuse me
sumimasen
すみません

please can you help me
taskete kudasai
助けて下さい

I am looking for this address *(point to written address)*
kono jūsho made ikitai dess ga
この住所まで行きたいのですが

where's the nearest...?
ichiban chikai ... wa doko dess ka?
一番近い … はどこですか？

is it far?
tōi dess ka?
遠いですか？

how do I get there?
dō ikeba ī dess ka?
どう行けばいいですか？

how many kilometres is it?
nan kiro dess ka?
何キロですか？

please draw me a map
chizu o kaite kudasai
地図を書いて下さい

how do I get to the ...?
... niwa dō ikeba ī dess ka?
… にはどう行けばいいですか？

park	**temple**	**shrine**
kōen	o-tera	jinja
公園	お寺	神社

we're lost
michi ni mayoimashta
道に迷いました

we're looking for ...
... o sagashte imass
… を探してます

answers – Asking the Way

- If you are meeting someone, arrange to meet at a prominent building or in a hotel lobby.
- Note that **furonto** in Japanese means the front desk and not the front of the hotel.
- If you are completely lost, phone the Japan Help-Line 0120 461 997. This is a freephone number.
- Shopkeepers or policemen in the local police box (**koban**) may be able to help if you show them the written address.

east	west	north	south	exit	entrance
higashi	nishi	kita	minami	deguchi	iriguchi
東	西	北	南	出口	入口

central exit/entrance
chūō deguchi/iriguchi
中央出口/入口

keep going straight ahead
mas-sugu itte kudasai
真っ直ぐ行ってください

the first	the second	on the right	on the left
saisho o	tsugi o	migi ni	hidari ni
最初	次を	右に	左に

you have to turn round
hiki kaeshte kudasai
引き帰してください

keep going		as far as …	as far as the church
sono mama susunde kudasai		… made	kyōkai made
そのまま進んでください		… まで	教会まで

turn left	turn right
hidari ni	migi ni
左に	右に

Bus

● On some buses you enter at the front and pay as you enter.
● On others you enter by a middle door, taking a ticket from a machine either side of the door. This has a number on it. A display board at the front of the bus tells you your fare when you get off. A machine near the driver gives change.
● Display boards show the next bus (in **kanji**). Write down your destination so that you can recognize it. The name of the next stop is also displayed electronically inside the bus.

does this bus go to …?
kono bass wa … ni ikimass ka?
このバスは … に行きますか？

I want to go to …
… ni ikitai dess
… に行きたいです

how long does it take by bus?
bass de dono kurai kakarimass ka?
バスでどのくらいかかりますか？

is the next bus stop …?
tsugi no bass tei wa … dess ka?
次のバス停は … ですか？

please tell me when we're at …
… ni tsuitara, oshiete kudasai
… についたら教えてください

please let me get off
sumimasen, oroshte kudasai
すみません 降ろして下さい

sorry, I forgot to take a ticket (on entering bus)
sumimasen, seiriken o torimasen deshta
すみません、整理券を取りませんでした

I got on at …
… kara norimashta
… から乗りました

Underground & Train

- *Don't sit on the 'silver seats' marked in Japanese and English. These are reserved for the elderly and disabled.*
- *Many stations are multistorey and link with shopping malls, so there are many levels which can be confusing.*
- *Avoid the rush hour crush (7–9am and 5–8pm). There are women-only carriages to avoid any danger of groping hands.*
- *Don't put your feet on seats, and eating and drinking is forbidden on public transport (both on trains and in the station).*

where is the subway station?
chikatets no eki wa doko dess ka?
地下鉄の駅はどこですか？

do you have an underground map?
chikatets no chizu wa arimass ka?
地下鉄の地図はありますか？

I want to go to …
… e ikitai dess
… へ行きたいです

can I go by underground?
chikatets de ikemass ka?
地下鉄でいけますか？

do I have to change?
norikaemass ka?
乗り換えますか？

where?
doko dess ka?
どこですか？

which line is it for …?
… yuki wa nan-ban sen dess ka?
… 行きは何番線ですか？

what's the next stop?
tsugi no eki wa nan dess ka?
次の駅はなんですか？

which station is it for Ueno?
ueno ni iku ni wa dono eki dess ka?
上野に行くには、どの駅ですか？

how do I buy a ticket? (from machine)
dō yatte kipp o kaeba ī dess ka?
どうやって切符を買えばいいですか？

I'm going to …
… e ikimass
… へ行きます

Train

● *The Japan Rail Pass represents fabulous value for money. It is available to overseas visitors but a voucher for it must be purchased outside Japan (visit www.japanrailpass.net for more details).*
● *Passes are available for one, two or three weeks.*
● *The pass starts operating from the minute you exchange the voucher. So if you plan to spend four weeks in Japan but want to travel only the first and last weeks, buy two separate week passes.*

where is the station?
eki wa doko dess ka?
駅はどこですか？

to the station please
eki made onegai shimass
駅までお願いします

where is the ticket office?
kipp uriba wa doko dess ka?
切符売り場はどこですか？

how much does it cost to ...?
... made ikura dess ka?
... までいくらですか？

I'm going to ...
... e ikimass
... へ行きます

a single	**2 singles**	**a child's single**
katamichi	katamichi nimai	kodomo katamichi
片道	片道二枚	子供片道

a return	**2 returns**	**a child's return**
ōfku	ōfku nimai	kodomo ōfku
往復	往復二枚	子供往復

a single to Nara please
nara e katamichi kipp o kudasai
奈良へ片道切符をください

2 returns to Nara
nara e ōfku kipp nimai kudasai
奈良へ往復切符を二枚ください

1st class	**2nd class**	**smoking**	**non smoking**
ittō seki	nitō seki	kitsuen	kin-en
一等席	二等席	喫煙	禁煙

Train

- You can exchange the voucher at the JR office at Narita Airport and use the pass on the Narita Express to the centre of Tokyo.
- For local trains you would buy tickets at the automatic machines. You need to know the **kanji** for your destination and have some change. 200 and 100 yen are particularly useful. There is a route map on the ticket machine and the price to each destination shown under the name. Insert your money and get a ticket to that value (rather than to that destination).

do you have a train timetable?
jikoku-hyō wa arimass ka?
時刻表はありますか？

which is the platform for …?
…-yuki wa nan-ban-sen dess ka?
… 行きは何番線ですか？

is this the train for …?
kono densha wa … yuki dess ka?
この電車は … 行きですか？

does this train stop at …?
kono densha wa … de tomarimass ka?
この電車は … で止まりますか？

please tell me when we arrive at …
… ni tsuitara, oshiete kudasai
… についたら教えて下さい

where is the exit for …?
… e no deguchi wa doko dess ka?
… への出口はどこですか？

is this seat free?
kono seki wa aete-imass ka?
この席は空いてますか？

Taxi

● *Japanese taxis are safe, clean and metered – but very expensive. However, there is no need to tip.*
● *Most taxi drivers won't speak English, so have your destination written down in* **kanji**.
● *The driver operates the doors which open and close automatically. You leave by the kerbside, never into the traffic.*
● *You will be expected to load and unload your own luggage – the driver operates the boot lid automatically.*

where can I get a taxi?
takshī noriba wa doko dess ka?
タクシー乗場はどこですか？

please go to ...
... e itte kudasai
... へ行って下さい

here is the address
kore ga jūsho dess
これが住所です

please go here (point on map)
koko e itte kudasai
ここへ行って下さい

how much will it cost to ...?
... made wa ikura dess ka?
... まではいくらですか？

please can I have a receipt
reshīto o onegai shimass
レシートお願いします

please order me a taxi
takshī o yonde kudasai
タクシーを呼んでください

to the airport please
kūkō made onegai shimass
空港までお願いします

to the station please
eki made onegai shimass
駅までお願いします

how long will it take?
dono gurai kakarimass ka?
どのくらいかかりますか？

Boat

- Japan Railways (JR) run some ferry services and on certain routes the JR Rail Pass can be used.
- There is a good ferry network in Japan linking the various islands. Ferries can be used as an alternative to trains if you wish to travel between the islands and have time to spare. The cheapest form of accommodation on boats travelling overnight is to sleep on the communal **tatami** mat floor.
- Boat trips are common from coastal towns for dolphin-watching, etc.

do you have a timetable?
jikoku-hyō wa arimass ka?
時刻表はありますか？

1 ticket	**2 tickets**	**single**	**round trip**
chiketto ichimai	chiketto nimai	katamichi	ōfku
チケット一枚	チケット二枚	片道	往復

are there any boat trips?
kankō-sen wa arimass ka?
遊覧船はありますか？

how long is the trip?
kankō ni wa dono kurai jikan ga kakarimass ka?
遊覧にはどのくらい時間がかかりますか？

when is the next boat?
tsugi no fune wa nan-ji dess ka?
次の船は何時ですか？

when does the boat leave?
fune wa nan-ji ni demass ka?
船は何時にでますか？

when does the ferry leave?
ferī wa nan-ji ni demass ka?
フェリーは何時に出ますか？

Car – driving

● Visitors need an international driver's licence and their own.
● You drive on the left in Japan.
● The best roads are expressways (signposted in green). These are toll roads and expensive. Speed limits vary: 40kph for six lanes, elevated sections are 60kph, mountainous stretches 80kph. Always check the signage.
● Some service stations on expressways just have toilets and vending machines for drinks and snacks.

can I park here?
koko ni chūsha dekimass ka?
ここに駐車できますか？

where can I park?
doko ni chūsha dekimass ka?
どこに駐車できますか？

is there a car park?
chūsha jō wa arimass ka?
駐車場はありますか？

how long can I park here?
koko ni nan-jikan chūsha dekimass ka?
ここに何時間駐車できますか？

we're going to ...
... ni ikimass
... に行きます

we're going to Nara
nara ni ikimass
奈良に行きます

what's the best route?
dono rūto ga ichiban ī dess ka?
どのルートが一番いいですか？

how do I get onto the motorway?
doko kara kōsoku ni noreba ī dess ka?
どこから高速に乗ればいいですか？

which exit do I take for ...?
... e wa dono deguchi de orireba ī dess ka?
... へはどの出口で下りればいいですか？

petrol – Car

- Petrol is cheaper than in the UK and the major companies have petrol stations.
- There is no self-service at petrol stations. Several people will come up to your car. One will ask how much petrol you want, another will clean the windscreen and someone else will clean your ashtray. Once you are ready to leave, they will usually stop the traffic for you to get on to the main road!
- The word 'gasoline' is more widely understood than 'petrol'.

where is the nearest filling station?
ichiban chikai gasorīn stando wa doko dess ka?
一番近いガソリンスタンドはどこですか？

fill it up please
mantan de onegai shimass
満タンでお願いします

3000 yen's worth of petrol
gasorin o san-zen en bun
ガソリンを三千円分

that's my car (over there)
are ga watashi no kuruma dess
あれが私の車です

this is my car (right here)
kore ga watashi no kuruma dess
これが私の車です

where is the air line?
eya wa doko dess ka?
エアーはどこですか？

where is the water?
mizu wa doko dess ka?
水はどこですか？

please check ...
... o chekk shte kudasai
... をチェックして下さい

the tyre pressure
taiya no kuki-ats
タイヤの空気圧

the oil
oiru
オイル

the water
mizu
水

Car – problems

● The Japan Automobile Federation (JAF) is equivalent to the AA. Visit their website on **www.jaf.or.jp/e/index_e.htm**
● The JAF publishes a 'Rules of the Road' guide in English to help foreign drivers in Japan. These are available at JAF offices throughout Japan. Visit the website for addresses.
● If you break down, try to phone from an emergency roadside phonebox. This allows the JAF recovery service to pinpoint your location. Have ready the model, colour and registration of the car.

my car has broken down
watashi no kuruma ga kowaremashta
私の車が壊れました

what do I do?
dō sureba ī dess ka?
どうすればいいですか？

I'm on my own
watashi wa hitori dess
私は一人です

I have children in the car
kodomo ga kuruma ni imass
子供が車にいます

where is the nearest garage?
ichiban chikai shuri kōjō wa doko dess ka?
一番近い修理工場はどこですか？

is it serious?
hidoi kosho dess ka?
ひどい故障ですか？

can you repair it?
naosemass ka?
直せますか？

the car won't start
kuruma ga ugokimasen
車が動きません

I have a flat tyre
taiya ga panku shimashta
タイヤがパンクしました

the engine is overheating
enjin ga ōbahīto shimashta
エンジンがオーバーヒートしました

the battery is flat
batterī ga naku-narimashta
バッテリがなくなりました

have you got the parts?
pāts wa arimass ka?
パーツはありますか？

it's not working
ugokimasen
動きません

- *Car rental firms are normally found near railway stations. You can also book on-line with many of the big worldwide firms.*
- *Rental fees generally cover insurance and unlimited mileage.*
- *Half-day hires are available, but one-way rentals are expensive.*
- *Small cars are cheaper to rent and more practical for negotiating city traffic and narrow country lanes.*

where is the nearest car rental firm?
ichiban chikai rentakā no mise wa doko dess ka?
一番近いレンタカーの店はどこですか？

I'd like to rent a car
kuruma o karitai dess
車を借りたいです

for one day
ichi nichi de
一日で

for a week
isshūkan de
一週間で

I would like a small car
kogata-sha ga hoshī dess
小型車が欲しいです

I would like a large car
ōgata-sha ga hoshī dess
大型車が欲しいです

I would like to rent this car
kono kuruma o karitai dess
この車を借りたいです

please explain the controls
sōsa o setsumei shte kudasai
操作を教えて下さい

what do we do if we break down?
moshi kowaretara dō sureba ī dess ka?
もし壊れたらどうすればいいですか？

when must I return the car by?
itsu made ni kuruma o kaeseba ī dess ka?
いつまでに車を返せばいいですか？

Shopping

● *Shopping is a national pastime in Japan!*
● *Shops are open 7 days a week from 10am to 8pm.*
● *Department stores close slightly earlier on Sundays. They offer free gift-wrapping services.*
● *Japanese value hand-made goods very highly – they also cost significantly more. Prices of simple items may shock you.*
● *VAT on shopping will be refunded at the airport if you complete the necessary forms.*

do you sell ...?
... wa arimass ka?
... はありますか？

stamps
kitte
切手

where can I buy ...?
... wa doko de kaemass ka?
... はどこで買えますか？

postcards
e-hagaki
絵葉書

films
firumu
フィルム

10 stamps
kitte jumai
切手十枚

for postcards
e-hagaki no
絵葉書の

to Britain
igiriss made
イギリスまで

a colour film
kara-firumu
カラーフィルム

a tape for this video camera
kono bideo camera no tāpe
このビデオカメラのテープ

when does the shop open?
mise wa nan-ji ni akimass ka?
店は何時に開きますか？

when does the shop close?
mise wa nan-ji ni shimarimass ka?
店は何時に閉まりますか？

I'm looking for a present
prezento o sagashte imass
プレゼントを探しています

please show me that
sore o misete kudasai
それを見せて下さい

this
kore
これ

that (by you)
sore
それ

that (over there)
are
あれ

Shopping

- Cameras, radios, etc. will often be cheaper in Japan and you usually find the latest designs, often months ahead of UK release dates. However, be warned that the instructions are often only in Japanese.
- You can buy wonderful gifts from local malls, supermarkets and 100-yen stores. (This will appal your Japanese friends!)
- It is generally difficult to find large sizes of clothes and shoes for men and women.

how much does this cost?
kore wa ikura dess ka?
これはいくらですか？

please write down the price
nedan o kaite kudasai
値段を書いて下さい

it's too expensive
takasugimass
高すぎます

I like this
kore ga ski dess
これがすきです

I don't like it
ski dewa arimasen
好きではありません

can I try it on?
shichaku dekimass ka?
試着できますか？

I'll buy this one
kore o kaimass
これを買います

please wrap it for me (regular)
tsutsunde kudasai
包んで下さい

please gift-wrap it for me
okurimono ni shte kudasai
贈り物にして下さい

please show me a ... one
... no o misete kudasai
... を見せて下さい

larger
motto ōkī
もっと大きい

smaller
motto chīsai
もっと小さい

newer
motto atarashī
もっと新しい

more expensive
motto takai
もっと高い

cheaper
motto yasui
もっと安い

Shopping – food

● *Vending machines are everywhere and very useful. You can get hot or cold tea, books, tights, etc. Ones selling alcohol shut down late at night until early morning.*

● *Most areas have a convenience store (**conbeni**) which is open 24 hours and sells just about everything.*

● *You can buy pre-packed **o-bentō** (lunchboxes), which come complete with disposable chopsticks, in most supermarkets. There are also shops selling **hoka hoka bentō** (these are hot lunchboxes).*

where can I buy...?
... wa doko de kaemass ka?
... はどこで買えますか？

fruit
kudamono
果物

bread
pan
パン

where is the supermarket?
sūpā wa doko dess ka?
スーパーはどこですか？

where is the baker's?
pan-ya wa doko dess ka?
パン屋はどこですか？

where is the market?
ichiba wa doko dess ka?
市場はどこですか？

which day is the market?
ichiba wa itsu arimass ka?
市場はいつありますか？

a litre of ...
... o ichi littōru
... 一リットル

milk
gyūnyū
牛乳

beer
bīru
ビール

water
mizu
水

a bottle of ...
... ippon
... 一本

wine
wain
ワイン

beer
bīru
ビール

water
mizu
水

a can of ...
... kan
... 缶

coke
kōra
コーラ

beer
bīru
ビール

water
mizu
水

a packet of ...
... wan-pak
... 1パック

iscuits
bisketto
ビスケット

sugar
satō
砂糖

food – Shopping

- *You must be over 20 to buy cigarettes and alcohol in Japan.*
- *Most food sold at supermarkets is pre-weighed and pre-wrapped. You just choose what you want and take it to the check-out.*
- *The fish market in Tokyo is well-worth visiting for the wonderful array of fish on display.*
- *The take-away counter at good supermarkets (and basements of department stores) can provide excellent, cheap meals.*

a kilo of …	**cheese**	**ham**
… ichi kiro	chīzu o	hamu o
… 一キロ	チーズ	ハム

200 grams of …	**butter**	**mince**
… ni-hyaku guram	batā o	minchi o
… 二百グラム	バター	ミンチ

potatoes	**apples**
jaga imo	ringo
ジャガイモ	りんご

8 slices of …	**ham**	**salami**
… o hachi mai	hamu	sarami
…を八枚	ハム	サラミ

a loaf of bread	**a baguette**
pan ikko	furans pan ippon
パン一個	フランスパン1本

a tin of …	**tomatoes**	**peas**
… no kan	tomato	gurīn pīs
… の缶	トマト	グリーンピース

a jar of …	**jam**	**honey**
… no bin	jamu	hachi-mits
… のビン	ジャム	蜂蜜

Sightseeing

● *The Japan National Tourist Organization website (**www.jnto.go.jp**) is excellent for practical information and for helping you find accommodation, transport, etc.*
● *Tourist Info Centers (TIC) have maps and leaflets in English.*
● *If you plan to go off the beaten track, book accommodation in advance – you're unlikely to find people who speak English.*
● *Entrance to museums and galleries is usually about US$10.*

excuse me, where is the tourist office?
sumimasen, ryokō annai-jo wa doko dess ka?
すみません、旅行案内所はどこですか？

where is the ...?
... wa doko dess ka?
... はどこですか？

museum	**castle**	**park**	**temple**	**shrine**
hakubutsu-kan	shiro	kōen	tera	jinja
博物館	城	公園	寺	神社

we want to visit ...
watashi tachi wa ... ikitai
私たちは ... 行きたい

have you any leaflets?
panfretto wa arimass ka?
パンフレットはありますか？

is it open to the public?
ippan kokai shteimass ka?
一般公開していますか？

how much is it to get in?
nyūjō-ryō wa ikura dess ka?
入場料はいくらですか？

is there a bus tour?
kankō-bass tsuā wa arimass ka?
観光バスツアーはありますか？

when does it leave?
itsu shuppats shimass ka?
いつ出発しますか？

where does it leave from?
doko kara demass ka?
どこから出ますか？

Sightseeing

- Beware of an overdose of temples and shrines! Particularly on guided tours.
- Major festivals are not the best times to travel around Japan. The transport system gets clogged up with people going home – particularly at Golden Week (end April/beginning of May, and **Obon** (mid-August).
- Public holidays falling on a Sunday are celebrated that day. The following Monday becomes a public holiday.

what time does the tour leave?
tsuā wa nan-ji ni shuppats shimass ka?
ツアーは何時に出発しますか？

are there reductions for ...?
... no waribiki wa arimass ka
... の割引はありますか？

students
gaksei
学生

children
kodomo
子供

seniors
rō-jin
老人

what time does it open?
nan-ji ni akimass ka?
何時に開きますか？

what time does it close?
nan-ji ni shimarimass ka?
何時に閉まりますか？

how much is the entry fee?
nyūjō-ryō wa ikura dess ka?
入場料はいくらですか？

where can I buy postcards?
doko de e-hagaki o kaemass ka?
どこで絵葉書を買えますか？

where can I buy souvenirs?
doko de o-miyage o kaemass ka?
どこでお土産を買えますか？

Sport & Leisure

- The Japan National Tourist Organization has details on sport. Visit their website **www.jnto.go.jp**.
- Some golf clubs welcome overseas visitors. Contact the JNTO for details. Golf is used to cement business relationships.
- You can practise your golf swing at a driving range. These are often multistorey or on the tops of buildings.
- Skiing in Japan is expensive – contact the JNTO for details.

where can we do ...?	**tennis**	**golf**
doko de ... ga dekimass ka?	tenis	gorufu
どこで ... ができますか？	テニス	ゴルフ

riding	**fishing**
jōba	tsuri
乗馬	釣り

where can we go hiking?
doko de haikingu ga dekimass ka?
どこでハイキングができますか？

do I need walking boots?
tozan-kutsu ga hitsuyō deshō ka?
登山靴が必要でしょうか？

where can we go swimming?
doko-ka oyogēru tokoro wa arimass ka?
どこか泳げるところはありますか？

where can we play golf?
doko de gorofu ga dekimass ka?
どこでゴルフができますか？

can we rent the equipment?
yōgu wa rentāru dekimass ka?
用具はレンタルできますか？

Sport & Leisure

- **Sumo** is a hugely popular spectator and tv sport. It takes place in different cities across Japan. If you are staying in a city hosting a tournament it is worth visiting the **Sumo Beya** (literally 'stable') where you can see the wrestlers practise.
- You can generally swim in the sea from July to mid-August. From mid-August the coastal waters become infested with jellyfish.
- You need a swimming cap in public pools.

can I hire …?
… kariremass ka?
… 借りれますか？

rackets
raketto
ラケット

golf clubs
gorufu kurab
ゴルフクラブ

I am a beginner
shoshinsha dess
初心者です

how much is it per hour?
ichi-jikan de ikura dess ka?
一時間でいくらですか？

how much is it per day?
ichi-nichi de ikura dess ka?
一日でいくらですか？

is there a soccer match?
sakkā no shiai wa arimass ka?
サッカーの試合はありますか？

where do I buy tickets?
chiketto wa doko de kaemass ka?
チケットはどこで買えますか？

can we take lessons?
ressun o ukeremass ka?
レッスンを受けれますか？

where is there a sports shop?
supōtsu ten wa doko dess ka?
スポーツ店はどこですか？

Nightlife

● *Major tour operators run fixed-price night tours to the more expensive nightclubs and cabarets. Ask at the Tourist Information Center.*
● *Cherry blossom time is when people go to the parks (usually at night) to admire the blossom and drink alcohol.*
● *To be sure of prices, stick to bars run by the big brewery firms. These include **Suntory**, **Nikka** and **Kirin**.*
● *Beware of cover charges which can be very expensive.*

what is there to do at night?
yoru asoberu tokoro wa arimass ka?
夜遊べるところはありますか？

which is a good bar?
ī bar wa doko dess ka?
いいバーはどこですか？

is it expensive?
soko wa takai dess ka?
そこは高いですか？

which is a good disco?
ī disko wa doko dess ka?
いいデイスコはどこですか？

where can we hear live music?
doko de raibu ongaku ga kikemass ka?
どこでライブ音楽が聞けますか？

are there any concerts?
konsāto wa arimass ka?
コンサートはありますか？

we want to go to a karaoke bar
karaoke ni ikitai dess
カラオケに行きたいです

are there any local festivals?
jimoto no matsuri wa arimass ka?
地元の祭りはありますか？

Nightlife

- **Karaoke** bars are very popular. Don't refuse a turn at the microphone if you are asked! You might find that what you think is an hour in a karaoke booth, turns out to be five.
- Visit **www.jnto.go.jp** for information on local festivals. The big festival (**Obon**) in the Tokyo area takes place in mid-July and there are often impressive firework displays.
- Prices for the theatre and for concerts tend to be high. You should dress quite conservatively.

we'd like to go to the ...	theatre	opera
... ē ikitai dess	gekijō	opera
... へ行きたいです	劇場	オペラ

ballet	a concert
balay	konsāto
バレー	コンサート

what's on?
ima nanika moyōshi wa arimass ka?
今何か催しはありますか？

do I need to book?	**how much are the tickets?**
yoyaku ga irimass ka?	chiketto wa ikura dess ka?
予約が要りますか？	チケットはいくらですか？

2 tickets ...	for tonight	for tomorrow night
... chiketto nimai	konya no	ashta no yoru no
... チケット二枚	今夜の	明日の夜の

for 5th August
hachi-gats itsuka no
8月5日の

when does the performance end?
kono kōen wa itsu owarimass ka?
この公演は何時終りますか？

Hotel

● The Japan National Tourist Organization and Tourist Information Centers can help with finding accommodation. Visit *www.jnto.go.jp*.
● Japan offers a wide choice of places to stay – from western-style hotels to traditional inns (**ryokan**).
● Capsule hotels comprise tiny, self-contained cubicles stacked on top of each other, with shared bath facilities. There are vending machines for food, drink and toiletries. They are good value.

where is the nearest hotel?
ichiban chikai hoteru wa doko dess ka?
一番近いホテルはどこですか？

have you a room for tonight?
konya heya wa arimass ka?
今夜部屋はありますか？

single	**double**	**family room**
shinguru	dabul	famirī rūm
シングル	ダブル	ファミリールーム

with bath	**with shower**
bāss tsuki	shawā tsuki
バス付	シャワー付

I/we will be staying ...	**one night**	**2 nights**	**3 nights**
... shimass	ippak	nihak	sanpak
... します	一泊	二泊	三泊

how much is it per night?
ippak ikura dess ka?
一泊いくらですか？

is breakfast included?
chōshoku komi dess ka?
朝食込みですか？

can I/we stay for 2 hours at this hotel?
ni-jikan dake taisoku wa dekimass ka?
二時間だけ休憩はできますか

Hotel

- *'Love hotels' should not be thought of as sleazy. They allow Japanese couples (even married ones) some privacy. Rooms are hired for 2-hour periods in the day or for overnight stays. Rooms can be wonderfully decorated on fanciful themes!*
- *A ryokan is a traditional Japanese inn. The price usually includes dinner and breakfast.*
- *A minshuku is a cheaper version of a ryokan, usually bigger and only in main tourist areas.*

I booked a room
heya o yoyak shteimass
部屋を予約しています

my name is ...
... dess
... です

my key please
kagi o kudasai
カギを下さい

come in!
haitte kudasai
入ってください

please come back later
ato de kite kudasai
後で来て下さい

please call me ...
... yonde kudasai
... 呼んで下さい

at 7 o'clock
shichi-ji ni
7時に

is there a laundry service?
kurīningu sābis wa arimass ka?
クリーニングサービスはありますか？

I'm leaving tomorrow
asu shuppats shimass
明日出発します

the bill please
o-kanjō o onegai shimass
お勘定をお願いします

when is check-out time?
chekk-aut wa itsu dess ka?
チェックアウトはいつですか？

Self-catering

● *Voltage throughout Japan is 100 volts.*
  ● *A transformer is required for any electrical appliances you take with you.*
  ● *Plugs are two-pronged.*
  ● *Rubbish must be separated into biodegradable, plastic, glass, tin, etc. Large items (e.g. furniture) can be put out once a month for collection.*
● *Visit www.jnto.go.jp for more information.*

which is the key for this door?
dore ga kono doā no kagi dess ka?
どれがこのドアのカギですか？

please show us how this works
kore ga dō sureba yoi no ka oshiete kudasai
これはどうすればよいのか教えて下さい。

who do I contact if there are any problems?
mondai ga aru toki doko e renrak sureba ī dess ka?
問題がある時どこへ連絡すればいいですか？

we need extra ...	**cutlery**	**sheets**
... o yobun ni kudasai	naifu to fōku	sheets
... を余分にください	ナイフとフォーク	シーツ

the gas has run out
gass ga kiremashta
ガスが切れました。

what do I do?
dō sureba ī dess ka?
どうすればいいですか？

where is the launderette?
koin randorī wa doko dess ka?
コインランドリーはどこですか？

where do I put the rubbish?
gomi wa doko ni okeba ī dess ka?
ゴミはどこに置けばいいですか？

Camping & Caravanning

● Official campsites are often only open during the Japanese camping season (July to August) and may be very full – visit www.outdoorjapan.com for information.

● The wet season in Japan is from early June to mid-July. The weather is hot and very muggy, causing clothes and books to get mouldy.

● It is always advisable to carry a small towel with you at all times and some water.

we're looking for a campsite
kyanpu-jo o sagashtemass
キャンプ場を探してます

have you a list of campsites?
kyanpu-jo no risto wa arimass ka?
キャンプ場のリストはありますか？

where is the campsite?
kyanpu-jo wa doko dess ka?
キャンプ場はどこですか？

have you any vacancies?
aki wa arimass ka?
空きはありますか？

how much is it per night?
ippak ikura dess ka?
一泊いくらですか？

we'd like to stay for ... nights
... pak shtai dess
... 泊したいです

can we have a more sheltered site?
motto kaze no ataranai basho wa arimass ka?
もっと風の当たらない場所はありますか？

this site is very muddy
koko wa totemo nukarunde imass
ここはとてもぬかるんでいます

is there another site?
hoka no tokoro wa arimass ka?
他の所はありますか？

is there a shop on the site?
o-mise wa arimass ka?
お店はありますか？

can we camp here?
koko de kyanpu dekimass ka?
ここでキャンプできますか？

Children

- *Children between six and eleven pay half price on rail fares. There is also a child Japan Rail Pass.*
- *www.tokyowithkids.com has useful info.*
- *Children under six travel free on trains. However, if the train is crowded, they should sit on your lap.*
- *Japanese school children wear a distinctive 'sailor-type' uniform with hats.*
- *Older Japanese children have all the latest gadgets.*

a child's ticket
kodomo no chiketto
子供のチケット

he/she is ... years old
kare /kanojo wa ... sai dess
彼は/彼女は ... 歳です

is there a reduction for children?
kodomo waribiki wa arimass ka?
子供割引はありますか？

do you have a children's menu?
kodomo-yō menyū arimass ka?
子供用メニューありますか？

what is there for children to do?
nani ka kodoma ga tanoshimeru mono wa nai deshō ka?
何か子供が楽しめるものはないでしょうか？

do you have ...? | **a high chair** | **a cot**
... arimass ka? | baby cheyā | baby bed
... ありますか？ | ベビーチェヤー | ベビーベッド

I have two children
kodomo ga futari imass
子供が二人います

do you have children?
kodomo ga imass ka?
子供がいますか？

is it safe for children?
kodomo ni anzen dess ka?
子供に安全ですか？

Special Needs

- Public transport in Japan caters for disabled travellers with numerous escalators and elevators. There are clear markings on platforms to assist the visually impaired.
- Stations have a Braille board with station names and fares.
- If you wish to use the elevator, you may have to find a member of staff to operate it.
- Check out the website **www.tokyoessentials.com/disabled.html** for information on accessibility to hotels, shopping and museums.

is it possible to visit ... with a wheelchair?
... ni kuruma-iss de ikemass ka?
... に車椅子で行けますか？

do you have toilets for the disabled?
shōgaisha-yō no toire ga arimass ka?
障害者用のトイレがありますか？

I need a bedroom on the ground floor
shinshitsu ga ikkai ni hoshii dess
寝室が一階に欲しいです

is there a lift?
erebētā ga arimass ka?
エレベーターはありますか？

where is the lift?
erebētā wa doko dess ka?
エレベーターはどこですか？

I can't walk far
tōku made arukemasen
遠くまで歩けません

are there many steps?
kaidan ga taksan arimass ka?
階段がたくさんありますか？

is there an entrance for wheelchairs?
kuruma-iss no iriguchi wa arimass ka?
車椅子の入口はありますか？

can I travel on this train with a wheelchair?
kono densha ni kuruma-iss de noremass ka?
この電車に車椅子で乗れますか？

Exchange Visitors

- These phrases are intended for families hosting Japanese-speaking visitors.
- If you receive a gift from a Japanese visitor, you should make a great fuss of it, expressing your delight at both its beautiful wrapping and contents.
- The Japanese are usually very quiet and self-effacing in public and dislike loudness and bad behaviour in others. It is probably worth keeping this in mind when you take any Japanese visitors out.

what would you like for breakfast?
chōshok wa nani ga ī dess ka?
朝食は何がいいですか？

what would you like to eat?
nani o tabetai dess ka?
何を食べたいですか？

what would you like to drink?
nani o nomitai dess ka?
何を飲みたいですか？

did you sleep well?
yoku nemuremashta ka?
よく眠れましたか？

would you like a shower?
shawā o tsukaimass ka?
シャワーを使いますか？

what would you like to do today?
kyō wa nani o shtai dess ka?
今日は何をしたいですか？

would you like to go shopping?
kaimono ni ikitai dess ka?
買い物に行きたいですか？

did you enjoy yourself?
tanoshimimashta ka?
楽しみましたか？

take care
ki o tskete
気をつけて

Exchange Visitors

- *These phrases are intended for those people staying with Japanese-speaking families.*
- *Japan runs a Home Stays scheme where you can stay in family homes. Visit the Japan National Tourist Organization at **www.jnto.go.jp** for more details.*
- *Always remove shoes when entering someone's home or before stepping on **tatami** matting.*
- *Don't use special toilet slippers in other parts of the house.*

I like…
watashi wa … ga ski dess
私は … が好きです

I don't like …
watashi wa … ga ski dewa arimasen
私は … が好きではありません

that was delicious
oishkatta dess
おいしかったです

thank you very much
arigatō gozaimashta
ありがとうございました

can I borrow …?
… o kariremass ka?
… を借れますか？

an iron
airon
アイロン

a hairdryer
heā doraiyā
ヘアドライヤー

what time do I have to get up?
nan-ji ni okinakereba narimasen ka?
何時に起きなければなりませんか？

can you take me by car?
kuruma de tsurete itte itadakemass ka?
車で連れて行って頂けますか？

how long are you staying?
dono gurai imass ka?
どのぐらいいますか？

I'm leaving in a week
isshūkan de shuppats shimass
一週間で出発します

thanks for everything
osewa ni narimashta
お世話になりました

I've had a great time
totemo tanoshikatta dess
とても楽しかったです

Bath

- *In a hotel you use a private bathroom as you would at home.*
- *If you are in someone's home, you must wash carefully before entering the bath. Soap should not get into the bathwater, which is often kept in the bath for days, with a mat on top to keep the heat in. Don't pull out the plug!*
- *A visit to an **onsen** (natual spring) or a **sento** (public bath) is a must. Here you shower at the shower stools before you go in, washing yourself very thoroughly before entering the water.*

may I take a bath?
o-furo ni haittemo ī dess ka?
お風呂に入ってもいいですか？

where is the bathroom?
o-furo wa doko dess ka?
お風呂はどこですか？

where is the toilet?
toire wa doko dess ka?
トイレはどこですか？

until when can I use the bath?
nan-ji made o-furo ni hairemass ka?
何時までお風呂に入れますか？

is it a mixed bath?
kon-yoku dess ka?
混浴ですか？

a large towel please
okī taoru o kudasai
大きいタオルをください

the water is very hot!
oyu wa totemo atsui dess!
お湯はとても熱いです

this is very relaxing!
totemo kimochi ga ī dess!
とても気持ちがいいです！

I like Japanese baths
nihon no o-furo ga ski dess
日本のお風呂が好きです

Complaints

- Japan is a very honest society. There is very little crime.
- Most Japanese people will try to help you as much as they can. Perhaps they are too helpful, in that they will try to give you directions even if they are not sure themselves where the place is.
- Japanese people dislike loud behaviour. Shouting or raising your voice would not be advisable in any situation, however frustrating it may be.

the light	**the air conditioning**	**... doesn't work**
denki	reibō	... ga tsukimasen
電気	冷房	... が動きません

there is no ...	**hot water**	**toilet paper**
... ga arimasen	oyu	toiretto pēpā
... がありません	お湯	トイレットペーパー

the room is dirty
heya ga kitanai dess
部屋が汚いです

the bath is dirty
ofuro ga kitanai dess
お風呂が汚いです

it is too noisy
urusai dess
うるさいです

the room is too small
heya ga semai dess
部屋が狭いです

this isn't what I ordered
chūmon to chigaimass
注文と違います

I want to complain
kujō o mōshitatemass
苦情を申し立てます

there is a mistake
machigai ga arimass
間違いがあります

this is broken
kore wa kowarete-imass
これは壊れてます

can you repair it?
kore o naosemass ka?
これを直せますか？

Problems

● *Though English is Japan's second language, few Japanese have encountered a native English speaker in person.*
● *Information and help is available from the local Tourist Information Centers. These are usually located in or near major railway stations or town centres. Look out for the red question mark with the word 'information' underneath.*
● *The Japan Help Line number is 0120 461 997. This is a freephone number.*

can you help me?
taskete kuremass ka?
助けてくれますか？

I don't speak Japanease
nihongo o hanasemasen
日本語を話せません

do you speak English?
eigo o hanashimass ka?
英語を話せますか？

does anyone speak English?
dareka eigo ga wakarimass ka?
誰か英語がわかりますか？

please speak slowly
yukkuri hanashte kudasai
ゆっくり話してください

I'm lost
michi ni mayotte shimaimashta
道に迷ってしまいました

I'm late
okuremass
遅れます

I need to get to ...
... ikanakereba narimasen
... 行かなければなりません

plane
hikōki
飛行機

flight connection
nori-tsugi
乗り継ぎ

I've missed my ...
... nori-okuremashta
... 乗り遅れました

my luggage has not arrived
nimots ga tsuitemasen
私の荷物が着いてません

Problems

- *If you are lost or need help, try asking a younger person for help. You might find an older person gets flustered.*
- *If you find that your spoken English is not understood, try writing it down clearly. Many Japanese have a good knowledge of written English.*
- *Ask the policeman in the local police box (**koban**) for help.*
- *As in any country, do not put yourself in danger. Do not leave valuables lying around and do be sensible.*

money	**passport**	**I've lost my ...**
okane	passpōto	... naku shimashta
お金	パスポート	... 無くしました

camera	**keys**
kamera	kagi
私のカメラ	私のカギ

I've left my bag in ...
... ni nimots o wasuremashta
... に荷物を忘れました

I have forgotten my ...
... o wasuremashta
... を忘れました

my ... is missing (thing)
watashi no ... ga naku-narimashta
私の ... がなくなりました

I have no money
okane ga arimasen
お金がありません

leave me alone!	**go away!**
watashi ni kamawanaide!	acchi e itte!
私に構わないで	あっちへ行って

Emergencies

- *The word for help is **taskete!***
- *There are often police boxes (**koban**) by main street crossings. They look after people in the street and help with directing them. They also receive lost property.*
- *If you have lost something, the chances are that you will get it back. Either go to the **koban** or ask at your hotel desk. If you have left something in a taxi, the driver will either take it back to your hotel or to the **koban**.*

help!
taskete!
助けて

can you help me?
taskete kuremass ka?
助けてくれますか？

there's been an accident
jiko ga arimashta
事故がありました

someone is injured
dareka ga kega o shimashta
誰かがケガをしました

call ...
... o yonde kudasai
... を呼んでください

the police
keisats
警察

an ambulance
kyū-kyū-sha
救急車

the fire brigade
shōbō tai
消防隊

he was driving too fast
kare wa spīdo o dashisugimashta
彼はスピードを出しすぎました

I need a report for my insurance
hoken no tame ni hōkokshō ga irimass
保険のために報告書が要ります

I've been robbed
tōnan ni aimashta
盗難に遭いました

Emergencies

- The emergency numbers are 110 for the police and 119 for an ambulance or the fire brigade.
- There are lots of small earthquakes and typhoons in Japan. You might only notice them by the trees bending a lot or from flights being postponed.
- Some public phones have a red emergency button.
- Tourist Information Centers provide details of English-speaking hospitals, dentists and pharmacies.

please call the police
keisats o yonde kudasai
警察を呼んでください

where is the nearest police station?
ichiban chikai kōban wa doko dess ka?
一番近い交番はどこですか？

I'm being followed
tsukerarete-imass
つけられています

I would like to call my embassy
taishikan ni denwa o shtai dess
大使館に電話をしたいです

where is the ... consulate
... ryōjikan wa doko dess ka?
... 領事館はどこですか？

British	**Australian**	**Canadian**	**New Zealand**	**US**
igiriss	ōstoraria	kanada	nyū jīrando	amerika
イギリス	オーストラリア	カナダ	ニュージーランド	アメリカ

I have no money
okane ga arimasen
お金がありません

Health

● Healthcare for visitors to Japan is expensive – make sure your travel insurance has adequate medical coverage for your stay.
● You can go to the out-patients department of a hospital for treatment. You will have to pay, probably in cash.
● You cannot usually get foreign medicine in Japan.
● Pharmacists are very good. If you act out your complaint, draw it, or point to the area in question, a product will be found or you will be sent to hospital.

have you something for ...?
... no tame ni nanika arimass ka?
... のために何かありますか？

flu
infurenza
インフルエンザ

diarrhoea
geri
下痢

is it safe to give children?
kore wa kodomo ni anzen dess ka?
これは子供に安全ですか？

I don't feel well
kibun ga yoku arimasen
気分が良くないです

I need a doctor
isha ni kakaritai dess
医者にかかりたいです

my son/daughter is ill
musuko/musume ga byōki dess
息子/ 娘 が病気です

he/she has a temperature
kare/kanojo wa nets ga arimass
彼/彼女　は熱があります

I'm taking this medicine
kono kusuri o nonde-imass
この薬を飲んでいます

I have high blood pressure
watashi wa kō-ketsu-atsu dess
私は高血圧です

I'm pregnant
ninshin shteimass
妊娠してます

I'm on the pill
piru o nonde-imass
ピルを飲んでいます

Health

- *Tap water is drinkable throughout Japan.*
- *Condoms are available in supermarkets, chemists and convenience stores.*
- *If you are put on antibiotics, make sure you get a full 10-day course and not the 5-day which seems favoured in Japan.*
- *Constipation is **bempi**. Ask for **bempi no kusuri**. You may need double the recommended dose since Japanese bodies are smaller than westerners'.*

I'm allergic to penicillin
penishirin ni arerugī ga arimass
ペニシリンのアレルギーがあります

my blood group is *(O, A etc.)* ...
ketsueki gata wa ... dess
血液型は ... です

I'm breastfeeding
junyū-chū dess
授乳中です

can I take it?
kore o nondemo ī dess ka?
これを飲んでもいいですか？

will he/she have to go to hospital?
kare/kanojo wa byōin ni ikanakereba narimasen ka?
彼/ 彼女は病院に行かなければなりませんか？

I need to go to A & E
kyū-kyū byōin ni ikitai dess
救急病院に行きたいです

where is the hospital?
byōin wa doko dess ka?
病院はどこですか？

I need to see a dentist
haisha ni ikitai dess
歯医者に行きたいです

I have toothache
ha ga itai dess
歯が痛いです

the filling has come out
tsume ga toremashta
詰物が取れました

it hurts
itai dess
痛いです

Business

で見

● To cement ties, present-exchanging is important. These presents are company to company and may well be displayed in the offices. They may also be person to person.
● Have business cards (**meishi**) printed with your details in English on one side and Japanese on the other.
● Treat **meishi** with respect, read them carefully on receipt and say the name out loud. Then put the card in your wallet to show that you are putting it somewhere safe and for future reference.

I'm ...
... dess
... です

here's my card
watashi no meishi dess
私の名刺です

I'm from Jones Ltd
watashi wa Jones-sha no mono dess
私はJones 社の者です

I'd like to arrange a meeting with Mr/Ms ...
...-san to o-ai shtai no de, yoyak o onegai shimass
...さんとお会いしたいので、予約をお願いします。

on 4 May at 11 o'clock
go-gats yokka no jū ichi-ji ni
5月4日の11時に

can we meet at a restaurant?
resutoran de aemass ka?
レストランでお会いできますか？

I will confirm by e-mail
e-mēru de kakunin shimass
メールで確認します

what's your e-mail address?
mēru adoress wa nan dess ka?
メールアドレスはなんですか？

is there a website?
hōmpēji wa arimass ka?
ホームページはありますか？

Business

- Never say 'no'. Use other expressions such as **tsugi ga warui** ('that might be troublesome').
- The Japanese don't speak in long monologues. They leave little spaces in conversation to ensure you are following. Nod encouragement in these spaces with **hai** or **dess ne**.
- Dress smartly and conservatively – suits for men, skirts for women. Women should always wear tights (even in the most humid weather), and never wear open sandal shoes for business.

I'm staying at Hotel …
hotel … ni taizai shteimass
hotel … に滞在してます

how do I get to your office?
anata no kaisha ē no michijun o oshiete kudasai
あなたの会社への道順を教えてください

here is some information about my company
kore wa tōsha no kaisha gaiyō dess
これは当社の会社概要です

I'm delighted to meet you
hajimemashte
初めまして

my Japanese isn't very good
watashi no nihongo wa umaku arimasen
私は日本語が上手くありません

I need an interpreter
tsūyak no kata o onegai shimass
通訳の方をお願いします

I would like some information about the company
kaisha annai o itadakemass ka?
会社案内を頂けますか？

Phoning

● Public phones accept 10-yen and 100-yen coins or phonecards.
It is best to use 10-yen coins for short calls as no refund is given
if you only partially use the 100-yen coin.
● Phonecards can be bought at vending machines, kiosks
and shops. There are cards for domestic use (which you just
insert), and international cards where you follow instructions.
● Calls are cheaper at night and Sat, Sun and national holidays.
● Numbers beginning 0120 and 0088 are freephone.

where can I buy a phonecard?
doko de terehon-kādo o kaemass ka?
どこでテレホンカードを買えますか？

a phonecard please
terehon kādo o kudasai
テレホンカードを下さい

I want to make a phone call
denwa o kaketai dess
電話をかけたいです

can I speak to ...?
... wa irasshaimass ka?
... はいらっしゃいますか？

this is ...
watashi wa ... dess
私は ... です

Mr Tanaka please
Tanaka san o onegai shimass
田中さんをお願いします

I'll call back later
ato de kake-naoshimass
あとでかけ直します

do you have a mobile phone?
keitei denwa wa o-mochi dess ka?
携帯電話はお持ちですか？

what's your phone number?
denwa-bangō o oshiete kudasai
電話番号を教えてください

Phoning

- You can make international phone calls from some public phones (look out for the international and domestic signs).
- Foreign mobiles won't work in Japan. You can hire mobile phones for your stay from Narita and Kansai airports.
- Direct calls can be made using a telephone company and dialling their access code. You can also use a credit card but you have to insert a 100-yen coin to dial the access company. The coin is then refunded.

this is my phone number
kore ga watashi no denwa-bangō dess
これが私の電話番号です

hello!
moshi-moshi!
もしもし

this is …
… dess
… です

may I speak to Mr/Mrs/Ms …
…-san o onegai shimass
… さんを　お願いします

I'll call back later
ato de kake-naoshimass
後でかけ直します

please speak more slowly
mō sukoshi yukkuri hanashte kudasai
もう少しゆっくり話してください

please repeat that
mō ichi-do itte kudasai
もう一度言ってください

who is calling?
donata dess ka?
どなたですか？

please hold a moment
shō-shō o-machi kudasai
少々お待ちください

please try again later
ato de o-kake-naoshi kudasai
あとでおかけ直しください

Post Office

- The Japanese mail system is efficient but fairly expensive.
- Post offices are open 9am–5pm, Mon–Fri. Some main post offices are open seven days a week.
- You can change money at large post offices.
- Letters can be addressed in **romaji** (western letters), but write clearly in block capitals.
- Mailboxes are red. If they have two slits, one is for local mail, the other for elsewhere.

where is the nearest post office?
ichiban chikai yūbin-kyok wa doko dess ka?
一番近い郵便局はどこですか？

by airmail please
kōkūbin de onegai shimass
航空便でお願いします

by registered mail please
kakitome de onegai shimass
書留でお願いします

aerogrammes please
kōkū shokan o kudasai
航空書簡を下さい

stamps please
kitte o onegai shimass
切手を下さい

postcards please
postokādo o onegai shimass
絵葉書を下さい

I want to send this parcel
kono ko-zutsumi o okuritai dess
この小包みを送りたいです

to Europe
yōroppa e
ヨーロッパへ

to Australia
ōstoraria e
オーストラリアへ

to America
amerika e
アメリカへ

how much will it cost?
ikura dess ka?
いくらですか？

how long will it take?
dono gurai kakarimass ka?
どのぐらいかかりますか？

E-mail & Fax

- *Japanese website addresses end **.jp**. Unless your computer is set up to read Japanese, you won't be able to read it.*
- *'At' is used for the symbol @.*
- *The pronunciation for 'at' is **atto**.*
- *www. is said as in English.*
- *The international dialling code for Japan is 0081.*
- *English web addresses are understood.*

I want to send an e-mail
e-mēru o okuritai dess
eメイルを送りたいです

what's your e-mail address?
anata no mēru adoress o oshiete kudasai
あなたのメールアドレスを教えてください

my e-mail address is ...
watashi no mēru adoress wa ... dess
わたしのeメイルアドレスは ... です

did you get my e-mail?
watashi no e-mail wa todokimashta ka?
私のメールは届きましたか？

I want to send a fax
fax o okuritai dess
faxを送りたいです

do you have a fax?
fax wa arimass ka?
faxはありますか？

what is your fax number?
fax bangō o oshiete kudasai
fax番号を教えてください

Numbers

- You will see roman numerals used for prices, etc.
- Before contact with China (about 1500 years ago), Japan had no written language. They counted from one to ten only and the words for these numbers are still in daily use, along with the Chinese-derived ones.
- Using numbers to count people and things is complicated, since they alter according to what is being counted.
- Keep pen and paper handy for writing down numbers.

	Chinese-derived form		**original Japanese form**	
0	零	rei		
1	一	ichi	一つ	hitots
2	二	ni	二つ	futats
3	三	san	三つ	mitts
4	四	yon or shi	四つ	yotts
5	五	go	五つ	itsuts
6	六	rok	六つ	mutts
7	七	shichi or nana	七つ	nanats
8	八	hachi	八つ	yatts
9	九	kyū or ku	九つ	kokonots
10	十	jū	十	tō

Beyond this only the Chinese-derived characters are in use:

11	十一	jū-ichi
12	十二	jū-ni
13	十三	jū-san
14	十四	jū-yon or jū-shi
15	十五	jū-go
16	十六	jū-rok
17	十七	jū-nana or jū-shichi
18	十八	jū-hachi

19	十九	jū-ku *or* jū-kyū
20	二十	ni-jū
21	二十一	ni-jū-ichi
22	二十二	ni-jū-ni
30	三十	san-jū
40	四十	yon-jū
50	五十	go-jū
60	六十	roku-jū
70	七十	nana-jū *or* shichi-jū
80	八十	hachi-jū
90	九十	kyū-jū
100	百	hyak
110	百十	hyaku-ichi
200	二百	ni-hyak
300	三百	sam-byak
500	五百	go-hyak
1000	千	sen
2000	二千	ni-sen
10,000	百千	ichi-man
1 million	百万	hyaku-man

Days & Months

● In Japanese, dates tend to be written in year, month, day form. So 17 August 2004 will be 2004.8.17.
● Months are literally, January = '1-month', February = '2-month', March = '3-month' and so on.
● Japan has four marked seasons: spring (March–May), when the cherry blossom is out; summer (June–August), when it gets very muggy; Autumn (Sep–Nov), usually dry with clear skies; and winter (Nov–Feb), which can be snowy on the mountains.

2004 ni-sen yo-nen 二千四年
2005 ni-sen go-nen 二千五年

what is the date?
kyō wa nan-nichi dess ka?
何日ですか？

which day?
nan nichi?
何日？

which month?
nan gats?
何月？

March 5th
go gats itska
五月五日

July 6th
roku gats muika
六月六日

Saturday
doyōbi
土曜日

on Saturdays
doyōbi niwa
土曜日には

every Saturday
maishū doyōbi
毎週土曜日

this Saturday
konshu no doyōbi
今週の土曜日

next Saturday
raishū no doyōbi
来週の土曜日

last Saturday
senshū no doyōbi
先週の土曜日

please can you confirm the date
hinichi o kakunin shte kudasai
日にちを確認してください

Days & Months

Monday	getsu-yōbi	月曜
Tuesday	ka-yōbi	火曜
Wednesday	sui-yōbi	水曜
Thursday	moku-yōbi	木曜
Friday	kin-yōbi	金曜
Saturday	do-yōbi	土曜
Sunday	nichi-yōbi	日曜

January	ichi-gats *(lit: '1 month')*	一月
February	ni-gats *('2 month')*	二月
March	san-gats *('3 month')*	三月
April	shi-gats *('4 month')*	四月
May	go-gats *('5 month')*	五月
June	roku-gats *('6 month')*	六月
July	shichi-gats *('7 month')*	七月
August	hachi-gats *('8 month')*	八月
September	ku-gats *('9 month')*	九月
October	jū-gats *('10 month')*	十月
November	jū-ichi-gats *('11 month')*	十一月
December	jū-ni-gats *('12 month')*	十二月

Time

- Japan is 9 hours ahead of Greenwich Mean Time.
- Japan is 14 hours ahead of New York and Toronto.
- Japan is 1 hour behind Australia.
- Shops generally open 10am–8pm, seven days a week. Department stores close earlier on Sundays.
- Office hours are 9am to 5pm, Mon–Fri.
- Times are generally written using the 24-hour clock.

what's the time? nan-ji dess ka? 何時ですか？	**am** go-zen 午前	**pm** go-go 午後
1 o'clock	ichi-ji 一時	
2 o'clock	ni-ji 二時	
3 o'clock	san-ji 三時	
4 o'clock	yo-ji 四時	
5 o'clock	go-ji 五時	
6 o'clock	roku-ji 六時	
7 o'clock	shichi-ji 七時	
8 o'clock	hachi-ji 八時	
9 o'clock	ku-ji 九時	
10 o'clock	jū-ji 十時	
11 o'clock	jū-ichi-ji 十一時	
12 o'clock	jū-ni-ji 十二時	
(noon)	shō-go 正午	
(midnight)	yo-naka 夜中	
8.15	hachi-ji jū-go-fun 八時十五分	
8.30	hachi-ji han 八時半	
8.45	hachi-ji-yon-jū-go-fun 八時四十五分	

when?
itsu?
いつ

when do you open?
nan-ji ni akimass ka?
何時に開きますか？

when do you close?
nan-ji ni shimemass ka?
何時に閉まりますか？

it is one o'clock
ichi-ji dess
一時です

it is three o'clock
san-ji dess
三時です

we arrived early
hayaku tsukimashta
早く着きました

we arrived late
okurete tsukimashta
遅れて着きました

soon
mamonaku
まもなく

at what time?
nan-ji ni?
何時に？

at mid-day
shōgo ni
正午に

at midnight
mayonaka ni
真夜中に

later
ato de
あとで

Holidays & Festivals

The traditional Japanese festival is called *matsuri*. Shintō belief is closely linked to the rice-growing cycle: prayers for a good harvest in the New Year, planting, harvesting and thanksgiving; while Buddhism places special importance on the remembrance of ancestors. The return of their spirits each midsummer is celebrated in the country-wide summer festivals (*natsu matsuri*) and *Obon*. In the Tokyo area this takes place during the middle of July, while in other parts of the country it tends to be the middle of August. Apart from the national festivals, there are many local *matsuri*. Ask the TIC for information.

Most public offices and many businesses are closed on national holidays. Shops are open (except for New Year). Public transport runs according to Sunday timetables but can be very crowded.

If a national holiday falls on a Sunday, it's celebrated that day, but the Monday also becomes a holiday. Christmas isn't an official holiday.

1-3 Jan	New Year *Families visit shrines, invite or visit friends or relatives*
2nd Mon Jan	Coming-of-age Day *Ceremonies for young people who turn 20.* **Kimono** *are often worn*
11 Feb	National Foundation Day
20-21 March	Spring Equinox
29 Apr-5 May	Golden Week
29 April	Green Day *The birthday of Emperor Shōwa*
3 May	Constitution Day
4 May	'Between Day' to bridge national holidays
5 May	Children's Day
3rd Mon July	Marine Day
3rd Mon Sep	Respect-for-the-aged Day
23-24 Sep	Autumn Equinox
2nd Mon Oct	Health-Sports Day
3 Nov	Culture Day
23 Nov	Labour Thanksgiving Day
23 Dec	Emperor's Birthday

Japanese Cuisine

Japanese traditional food consists of a few staple ingredients plus some side dishes. If necessary, food is cut into manageable bits before being served so that everything can be picked up easily with *hashi* (chopsticks). Try and practise with chopsticks before you arrive in Japan; it will increase your confidence. The word *gohan* means 'meal' as well as 'rice', which gives an idea of rice's importance.

Generally speaking, the eye stimulates the appetite in Japanese cuisine, whereas it is more the nose in western cooking. Furthermore, for many Japanese the concept of *shita-zawari,* (literally 'tongue-feel') is very important, especially in the case of *gohan* (boiled rice). This is the feel (not so much the actual taste) which the food has inside the mouth. For westerners, the 'feel' of toast in the mouth, with its crunchy exterior and soft interior may be akin to Japanese fussiness about the 'right' rice or *tofu* (bean curd).

Japanese are generally eclectic in their food tastes, and separate them into *nihon-ryōri* (Japanese cuisine), *seiyō-ryōri* (western cuisine), *chūka-ryōri* (Chinese cuisine) and *kankoku-ryōri* (Korean cuisine). You're unlikely to find authentic-tasting international cuisine apart from in very expensive foreign restaurants with imported non-Japanese chefs. Japanese attempts at western food look very good, but can taste rather bland.

Breakfast is either western-style – ham and eggs, toast and coffee, etc., or Japanese-style, such as *gohan* (rice), into which a raw egg is stirred. Side dishes are *miso* soup (from soy beans), *nattō* (fermented soy beans), *tsukemono* (pickles) and *nori* (seaweed), washed down with *o-cha* (green tea). Lunch, eaten between 12 and 1, is often noodles or sandwiches. Lunchboxes, *o-bentō*, are popular. Dinner (around 6pm) is when families eat together (although fathers might not arrive until much later in the evening during the week).

Eating places

FOOD IN JAPAN

You can find all types of eating places and foods in Japan. US-style fast food is popular. Visit **www.japan-guide.com** for an overview. And **www.bento.com** for a guide to eating out in Japan.

In traditional Japanese restaurants you find low tables and (often) *tatami* matting. You will have to remove your shoes so make sure your socks are respectable.

The less garish the establishment, the more traditional (and probably more expensive it will be).

COFFEE SHOP

service charge

A 10% service charge is generally included in the bill and there is no need to tip.

bill/check

The word for the bill or check is *kanjo*.

USEFUL WORDS

&

Just so you aren't stuck asking for one thing, the word for 'and' is pronounced like 'tot' but without the final 't'.

TRADITIONAL COFFEE SHOPS

Traditional coffee shops, known as *kissaten* (serving mostly non-alcoholic drinks and snacks) are good places to relax as you can linger for as long as you like.

The only problem is that they can become very smoky.

Most coffee shops and restaurants will automatically bring you a glass of tap water (which is safe to drink) and a small hand towel to wipe your face and hands.

COFFEE

Kissaten are popular meeting places to do business.

TEA

Coffee is *kōhī* and ordinary tea (not green tea) is *kōcha*.

Green tea is *ocha* and is usually drunk with Japanese meals. You generally don't have milk in it.

Eating places

VENDING MACHINES

Vending machines have all kinds of hot and cold snacks.

SASHIMI

Sashimi is slices of raw fish. *Sushi* is fish on rice. Men eat *sushi* after work rather like Spanish people eat tapas. Look out for the conveyor belt *sushi* (*kaitenzushi*), where the price is shown by the colour of the plate.

CONVENIENCE STORES

If you need a late-night snack, or don't want the hassle of going to a restaurant, you can buy micro-waveable snacks (such as pot noodles) in convenience stores.

Try acquiring a taste for rice balls (which you can buy at any convenience store). They can become addictive and filling.

Basements of department stores are good places for cheap food.

BREAKFASTS

In most local cafes you can get breakfast for about the price of a cup of coffee. Ask for a morning set (*morningu stetto, kudasai*). You will be given some choices. Ask for *kōhī* (coffee), *ocha* (green tea), *kōcha* (black tea), *o-sarada* for salad and *o-kudamono* for fruit. *Pan* is bread and *tosto* is toast.

DEPARTMENT STORES

Most department stores have a selection of eating places on different floors. *Ryon* is one of the many popular chains of eateries.

LUNCHTIME

Most restaurants offer a cheap *seto* (set meal) at lunchtime, but portions tend to be rather small.

Lunch on this menu board is from 10am–3pm.

You can buy pre-packed *o-bentō* (lunchboxes) in most supermarkets, station kiosks, etc. There are also shops selling *hoka hoka bentō* (hot lunchboxes).

Eating places

FISH MARKETS

There are markets selling most foods in Japan – from the fish markets in coastal cities which open in the early hours of the morning to stalls selling an assortment of sour pickles. It is worth trying to visit the fish market in Tokyo (*Tsukiji*) and sampling the *sushi* at one of the *sushi* counters. (They tend to look like dives, but don't be put off, ask around to find out which one is the best.) They often have a 2-option selection – one is around ¥ 2,500 and the other is ¥3,000. If you are an adventurous eater, go for the more expensive option, you'll taste fish you have never experienced elsewhere. Otherwise, if you just want to try some wonderful *sushi*, stick with the first option.

NOODLES

Noodles – Japanese fast food. People are very helpful in noodle shops. If you look anxious and try asking for beef or chicken, they will bring you a dish of food. Popular choices are chicken – *toriniku*, beef – *gyuniku*, squid – *ika*. It is worth learning the *kanji* characters for these so that you can spot them in a menu.

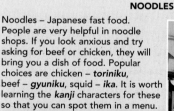

NOODLE SHOP MENU

NOODLE SHOP

BEER CHAINS

Beer (similar to German lager) is popular in Japan and often drunk with meals.

The big breweries in Japan include Suntory, Nikka and Kirin. They own chains of pub-type restaurants such as Lion's Beer Hall and Kirin City.

They are good places for inexpensive food. Women can feel quite at ease there.

The word for cheers is *kanpai!*

The equivalent to bon appétit is *itadakimass!*

PLASTIC FOOD

Many eating places in Japan have plates of plastic food on display to show customers what they offer.

When out with Japanese, it is the custom to pour drinks for other people at your table. Don't pour your own drink, wait until somebody does it for you. Take care if you drink quite quickly, you may find your glass being refilled more often than you would like.

Eating places

RESTAURANTS

Most restaurants have the menu and prices displayed outside. Many menus are also picture menus which means that you can see exactly what you are going to order.

Restaurants close quite early – between 10 and 11pm.

DIFFERENT CUISINES

Japanese like a wide range of different foods and separate them into *nihon-ryōri* (Japanese cuisine), *seiyo-ryōri* (western cuisine), *chūka-ryōrii* (Chinese cuisine) and *kankoku-ryōri* (Korean cuisine).

SPANISH RESTAURANT

STEAK HOUSE

ITALIAN RESTAURANT & MENU

SEAFOOD

RESTAURANTS

You may find the western food rather bland. Japanese people do not like highly spiced foods, so while the dishes look good, they might not be as tasty as you would expect.

KOREAN BARBECUE RESTAURANT

CHINESE RESTAURANT

Eating places

YAKITORI

These restaurants serve grilled chicken on skewers. They are usually lively places which are frequented by business men after work.

Check at the restaurant entrance what credit cards are accepted. Outside main cities you may find it more difficult to find places that have the facility to accept credit cards.

JAPANESE RESTAURANTS

Most Japanese restaurants will automatically bring chopsticks (*hashi*), but knives and forks are available on request.

Sushi bars can be quite intimidating. There is often no menu on the outside and you cannot see into most of them. Prices can vary enormously and it is hard to tell if you are going into a super expensive one. If the first price on the menu is around ¥200, then the place won't bankrupt you. Tea (*o-cha*) automatically comes free as does the pickled ginger (*gari*).

TEMPURA

Tempura is seafood and vegetables deep fried in *tempura* batter. It was originally brought to Japan by the Portuguese.

110

Eating places

RESTAURANTS OUTSIDE THE CITIES

In this traditional country restaurant the food is cooked over charcoal.

Raw fish is a delicacy in Japan. A freshly-killed fish might still twitch after death. Rather than being repulsed by this, Japanese see it as an indication of how fresh the fish is.

Sake is warmed in freshly-cut bamboo, giving it a wonderful aroma.

Green wasabi – Japanese horseradish can be breathtakingly hot. Approach with caution!

If you are keen to try out Japanese food, try telling your hosts that you love Japanese food, except for **nattō** (fermented beans eaten at breakfast). You either love **nattō** or hate it. This should convince your host that you must know enough about Japanese food to know whether you like **nattō** or not and they should feel confident ordering Japanese dishes for you, rather than steering you towards western restaurants.

A good expression to show your appreciation of the food is *oishī*. You should say it after the first mouthful.

Ordering drinks

● Cafés, which serve mostly non-alcoholic drinks and snacks, are a good place to relax as you can linger as long as you like.
● Cafés tend to be very smoky.
● *O-cha* is green tea and is drunk throughout the day. It is drunk without milk and is usually free with your meal.
● *Kōcha* is black tea (what you are probably more used to).
● Traditional coffee shops (**kissaten**) can be very expensive. They are often used as business meeting places.

may I have a black coffee
kōhī onegai shimass
コーヒーを下さい

may I have an American coffee *(not so strong)*
amerikan kōhī onegai shimass
アメリカンコーヒーお願いします。

may I have two cups of coffee
kōhī futats o onegai shimass
コーヒーを二つお願いします。

Indian tea	**green tea**
kō-cha	ō-cha
紅茶	お茶

may I have a tea with lemon
remon kō-cha onegai shimass
レモンティーお願いします。

may I have an iced coffee
aisu kōhī onegai shimass
アイスコーヒーお願いします

may I have an iced tea please
aisu tee onegai shimass
アイスティーお願いします

Ordering drinks

- When out with Japanese, it is the custom to pour drinks for other people at your table. Don't pour your own drink – wait until someone does it for you.
- Brewery-run bars such as Suntory, Nikka and Kirin sell beer and food. These are generally not too expensive.
- If you are out with Japanese business associates, watch out for the amount you drink. An empty glass calls out to be replenished. If you do find yourself worse for wear, try not to be loud and raucous.

may I have some mineral water
mineraru uōtā onegai shimass
ミネラルウオーターお願いします

2 bottles please
ni-hon onegai shimass
二本お願いします

do you have …?
… wa arimass ka?
… はありますか？

the wine list please
wain no menyū o kudasai
ワインのメニューを下さい

a bottle of red wine
aka wain o ippon
赤ワインを一本

a bottle of white wine
shiro wain o ippon
白ワインを一本

a glass of … wine	**red**	**white**
guras wain no …	aka	shiro
グラスワインの …	赤	白

would you like a drink?
nani ka o-nomi ni narimass ka?
何かお飲みになりますか？

what will you have?
nani ga yoroshī dess ka?
何がよろしいですか？

another round please
o-kawari o onegai shimass
お代わりをお願いします

cheers!
kanpai!
乾杯！

I've had enough thanks
mo kekkō dess
もう結構です

Ordering food

- Restaurants close early, between 10 and 11pm.
- Noodle shops are a good place to eat a quick meal. It is worth learning the **kanji** for chicken, beef, tomato, squid, etc.
- Most Japanese restaurants will bring you chopsticks, but knife, fork and spoon are available on request.
- Never leave chopsticks sticking in food, especially rice (it is a symbol of death).
- In some restaurants which use **tatami** you'll have to remove shoes.

may I/we enter?
haitte mo ī dess ka?
入ってもいいですか？

do you serve meals?
shoku-ji wa dekimass ka?
食事はできますか？

a table for … please
… no tēburu o onegai shimass
… のテーブルをお願いします

one/2/3
hitori-yō/futari-yō/san-nin-yō
一人用/二人用/三人用

please show me the menu
menyū o misete kudasai
メニューを見せてください

do you have a menu in English?
eigo no menyū wa arimass ka?
英語のメニューはありますか？

I'd like the set meal
teishok o kudasai
定食を下さい

the assorted set please (e.g. in the case of sushi)
moriawase o kudasai
盛り合わせを下さい

Ordering food

- Most restaurants automatically bring a glass of tap water (which is safe to drink) and a small hand towel (**oshibori**).
- Most restaurants offer a cheap **seto** (set meal) at lunchtime, but portions tend to be small.
- In most local cafés you can get breakfast for about the price of a cup of coffee. Ask for a morning set – **morningu setto kudasai**. Bread is **pan**, toast is **tosto**, salad is **o-sarada** and fruit is **o-kudamano**.

what do you recommend?
nani ga o-susume dess ka?
何がお勧めですか？

please choose for me
o-makase shimass
お任せします

I'll have this
kore o kudasai
これを下さい

I don't eat meat
nik wa tabemasen
肉は食べません

some more of … please
… o mō skoshi kudasai
… をもう少し下さい

do you have any vegetarian dishes?
bejitarian ryōri wa arimass ka?
ベジタリアン料理はありますか？

excuse me!
sumimasen
すみません

some water please
o-mizu o kudasai
パンを下さい

a knife and fork please
naifu to fōku o kudasai
ナイフとフォークを下さい

bon appetit!
itadakimass!
いただきます

thanks for the delicious meal
go-chisō-sama deshta
ごちそうさまでした

the bill please
o-kanjō o onegai shimass
お勘定をお願いします

shall we go Dutch?
warikan de ī dess ka?
割勘でいいですか

Special requirements

- There are very few vegetarian restaurants in Japan.
- Many restaurants have very limited selections of vegetarian dishes.
- Fruit can be rather expensive.
- The vinegared rice is regarded very highly so soy sauce is not poured on. Instead use it as a dip.
- Many Japanese dishes include raw fish. For this reason the fish has to be extremely fresh.

what is this?
kore wa nan dess ka?
これは何ですか？

I'm vegetarian
bejitarian dess
ベジタリアンです

I don't eat fish
sakana wa tabemasen
魚は食べません

I don't eat pork
buta-nik wa tabemasen
豚肉は食べません

I'm allergic to shellfish
watashi wa kai ni arerugī ga arimass
私は貝にアレルギーがあります

I am allergic to peanuts
watashi wa pīnats ni arerugī ga arimass
私はピーナッツにアレルギーがあります

I can't eat raw eggs
nama tamago wa tabemasen
生卵は食べません

is it raw?
sore wa nama dess ka?
それは生ですか？

I'm on a diet
daietto chū des
ダイエット中です

I don't drink alcohol
arukōru wa nomimasen
アルコールは飲みません

Menu reader

The following are the major staple foods:

gohan/meshi ご飯/めし	white, boiled rice, usually stickier than varieties from outside Japan
udon/soba うどん/そば	noodles

Dishes based mainly on rice include the following:

yaki-meshi 焼き飯	fried rice
sushi 寿司	rice balls with sliced raw fish
onigiri おにぎり	rice balls wrapped in seaweed
donburi どんぶり	various foods *(e.g. chicken, egg)* on top of a bowl of rice
inari-zushi いなり寿司	seasoned rice, wrapped in fried bean curd
karē raisu カレーライス	curry with rice

Dishes based on noodles include the following:

udon うどん	thick, white wheatflour noodles
soba そば	thin, brown buckwheat noodles
yaki-soba やきそば	fried buckwheat noodles with meat and vegetables

Menu reader

sōmen
ソーメン
thin, white wheatflour cold noodles

rāmen
ラーメン
Chinese-style noodles, often in 'instant' packs

Some of the more common words connected with vegetables and vegetable dishes are:

tōfu
豆腐
bean curd

shītake
しいたけ
mushrooms, Japanese-style

tsukemono
漬物
pickled vegetables

nori
のり
seaweed

daizu
大豆
soybeans

shōyu
醤油
soy sauce

nattō
納豆
fermented soybeans

miso
味噌
fermented paste of soybeans

yaki-imo
焼き芋
baked yams

Some Japanese words connected with fish are:

awabi
あわび
abalone

Menu reader

ebi えび	**shrimps**
fugu ふぐ	**blowfish** *(poison removed by licensed chefs)*
ika イカ	**squid**
kaki カキ	**oysters**
kani カニ	**crabs**
katsuo かつお	**bonito** *(e.g. dried bonito shavings on soup)*
koi 鯉	**carp**
maguro マグロ	**tuna**
tako タコ	**octopus**
tempura 天ぷら	**deep-fried seafood with vegetables**
unagi うなぎ	**eel** *(usually grilled)*

Meat

gyū-nik 牛肉	**beef**
suki-yaki すき焼き	**sliced beef with vegetables and raw egg, cooked at table**

Menu reader

teppan-yaki 鉄板焼き	sliced beef and vegetables, grilled at table
yaki-tori 焼き鳥	grilled chicken kebabs
rebā レバー	liver
kushi-kats 串かつ	meat and vegetables, deep-fried on skewers
buta-nik 豚肉	pork
katsudon かつドン	deep-fried pork on rice
tonkats とんかつ	deep-fried pork cutlets
gyōza 餃子	seasoned minced pork, stuffed into fried dumplings

DICTIONARY
English-Japanese

Dictionary abbreviations

(n) noun

(vb) verb

(adj) adjective

(adv) adverb

A

a, an *see* GRAMMAR
abroad kaigai (ni)
abscess nōyō
accelerator aksēru
to accept: *do you accept credit cards?*
kurejitto kādo demo ī dess ka?
accident *(traffic, etc)* jikō
  accident and emergency department
  kyūkyū-byōtō
accommodation shukuhaku
account *(bank)* kōza
ache itami
  my head aches atama ga itai dess
to act *(do)* shimass
actor haiyū
actress joyū
adaptor *(electrical)* adaptā
address jūsho
  what is the address? jūsho o oshiete
  kudasai
  what is your address? go-jūsho o
  oshiete kudasai
  this is my address watashi no jūsho dess
admission fee nyūjō-ryō
adult otona
advance: *in advance* maemotte
advance payment: sakibarai
advertisement senden
to advise: *what do you advise?* dō sureba
ī dess ka?
to afford: *I can't afford it* takasugimass
afternoon gogo
  in the afternoon gogo ni
  this afternoon kȳo no gogo
again mata
age *(person's)* toshi
  (time) jidai

Address

住所

Adult

大人

Afternoon

午後

Airline

Airport

Aomari

agenda *(for meeting)* kyōgi jikō
ago: *a week ago* isshūkan mae ni
to agree *(support a proposal):*
  I agree sansei shimass
  I don't agree sansei shimasen
  do you agree? sansei shimass ka?
to agree: *that's true, isn't it?* sō dess ne
  let's do that sō shimashō
aid *(charity)* enjo
AIDS eizu
air kūki
air conditioning reibō
  is there air conditioning? reibō ga
  arimass ka?
air pollution taiki osen
air hostess schuwādes
airline kōkū gaisha
airmail kōkūbin
airport kūkō
  airport bus kūkō bass
alarm *(in bank, shop)* keihō
alarm call mōningu kōru
  I'd like an alarm call at... ...ni mōningu
  kōru o onegai shimass
alarm clock mezamashi-dokei
alcohol arukōru
all subete (no)
allergic: *I'm allergic to shellfish* kai-rui no
  arerugī dess
allowed: *is it allowed?* ī dess ka?
alone hitori
  I'm travelling alone hitori-tabi dess
always itsumo
a.m. *(before noon)* gozen
ambassador taishi
ambulance kyū-kyū-sha
  please call an ambulance kyū-kyū-sha o
  yonde kudasai
America Amerika

123

American (adj) Amerika-no
  (person) Amerika-jin
amount gaku ; ryō
  small amount shōgaku ; shōryō
  large amount kōgaku ; tairyō
  total amount sōgaku ; sōryō
amusement park yūenchi
anaesthetic (n) masuizai
ancestor senzo
ancient kodai-no
and (furthermore) soshte
and to
angina angina ; kyōshinshō
angry okotteiru
animal dōbuts
ankle ashi-kubi
anniversary kinenbi
  wedding anniversary kekkon kinenbi
annoying: *it's very annoying* taihen
  meiwaku dess
annually maitoshi
another (a different kind) betsu no
  I'd like another betsu no mono ga
  hoshī dess
another (one more) mō hitots
  would you like another drink? mō ippai
  nomimass ka?
answer (written) henji
  (spoken) kotae
  there's no answer (on phone) daremo
  denwa ni demasen
answering machine russban denwa
antibiotic (n) kōsei busshits
antihistamine (n) kō-hisutamin-zai
antique (n) kottōhin
antiseptic (n) bōfuzai
anyone dare demo
anything nan demo
anywhere doko demo

April

四月

Arrival

到着

Art Gallery

ギャラリー

apartment apāto
apologies: *my apologies!* (formal) owabi
  itashimass
  (informal) gomen nasai
appendicitis mōchōen
appetite shokuyok
apple ringo
apple juice ringo jūs
application (job) mōshkomi
appointment yaksok
apricot anzu
April shi-gats
are: *are there any...?* ...ga arimass ka?
arm ude
armbands (for swimming) ude wa
to arrange: *can we arrange a meeting?*
  mīting o hiraitemo ī dess ka?
arrivals (airport) tōchak
to arrive tōchak suru
  I will arrive at 8 pm gogo hachi-ji ni
  tōchak shimass
art geijuts ; bijuts
art gallery bijuts-kan ; āto gyararī
arthritis kansets-en
artichoke ātichōku ; kikuimo
artificial jinkō
artist geijuts-ka
as: *as soon as possible* dekiru dake
  hayaku
ashtray haizara
Asia Ajia
to ask tazuneru
asparagus asparagass ; aspara
aspirin: *do you have any aspirin?* aspirin
  wa arimass ka?
assembly plant kumitate kōjō
assistant (shop) ten-in
asthma zensoku
  I get asthma zensoku dess

at: *at home* uchi de
  at 4 o'clock yoji ni
atmosphere *(of place)* funinki
attractive miryokuteki-na
aubergine nasu
audience *(theatre etc)* chōshū
August hachi-gatsu
aunt *(own)* oba
  (somebody else's) oba-san
Australia ōstoraria
Australian *(adj)* ōstoraria-no
  (person) ōstoraria-jin
author chosha
automatic *(car)* .mishon-sha
autumn aki
available: *when will it be available?*
  itsu goro dekimass ka?
avalanche nadare
avenue tōri ; namiki-michi
avocado abokado
to avoid sakeru
  what food should I avoid? donna
  tabemono o sakeru-beki dess ka?
away: *I will be away in August*
  hachi-gats wa russ dess
awful hidoi

B

baby aka-chan
baby food rinyūshoku
baby milk bebi miruku
baby seat bebi shīto
babysitter bebi-shittā
baby wipes oshiri fuki
bachelor dokshin
  I am a bachelor dokshin dess
back *(of body)* senaka
  (adv) when will he be back? (kare wa) itsu
  modorimass ka?

Bank

銀行

Basement

地下室

Bath

風呂

126

I'd like to go back modoritai dess
bad *(character, morally)* warui
  (food) kusatta
bag baggu ; kaban
baggage nimots
baggage reclaim tenimots hikitori-jo
baker's pan-ya
ball bōru
banana banana
band *(musical)* bando ; gakudan
bandage hōtai
bank ginkō
bar *(to drink in)* bā ; izakaya
  bar of chocolate choko bā
barbecue bābekyū
barber's toko-ya
bargain bāgen
  it's a bargain bāgen dess
baseball yakyū
baseball game yakyū no shiai
basement chika
basket kago
basketball baskettobōru
bath furo
bathroom yokushits
bath towel basu taoru
bath tub yokusō
battery *(for radio, etc)* denchi
  (for car) batterī
beach hama
bean *(soya)* mame
beancurd tōfu
beautiful utsukushī
  how beautiful! nante utsukushī!
bed *(western)* beddo
  (Japanese) toko
  double bed daburu beddo
  single bed shinguru beddo
bed and breakfast chōshoku-tski yado

bedding shingu
bedroom shinshits
  single (bedroom) hitori yō
  double (bedroom) futari yō
bee sting: *I've been stung by a bee*
  hachi ni sasareta
beef gyū-nik
beer bīru
  bottled beer bin bīru
  draught beer nama bīru
before ...mae ni
  before 4 o'clock yo-ji mae ni
  before next week konshu chū ni
to begin hajimeru
to belong to: *it/they belong(s) to me*
  watashi no mono dess
  does this belong to you? anata no mono
  dess ka?
belt beruto
beside: *can I sit beside you?* tonari ni
  suwatte ī dess ka?
best: *I like this best* kore ga ichiban
  ski dess
better yoi
bicycle jitensha
big ōkī
bigger: *have you anything bigger?* motto
  ōkī mono ha arimass ka?
bike jitensha
  mountain bike maunten baik
bill (o-)kanjō
  can I have the bill, please? (o-)kanjō
  onegai shimass
binoculars bōenkyō
bird tori
birthday tanjōbi
  happy birthday! tanjōbi omedetō!
birthday present tanjōbi prezento
biscuits bisketto

Bowl

椀

Box

箱

Breakfast

朝食

Bus

バス

Butcher's

肉屋

Cash

現金

bit: *just a bit* hon no skoshi
to bite kamu
bitter *(taste)* nigai
  it's too bitter for me nigasugimass
black *(n)* kuro
  (adj) kuroi
blanket mōfu
bleach hyōhakuzai
to bleed: *it won't stop bleeding* chi ga
  tomaranai
blind *(adj)* me no mienai
  (for window) braindo
blocked tsumatta
  the sink is blocked nagashi ga tsumatte
  imass
  my nose is blocked (watashi no) hana ga
  tsumatte imass
blood chi ; ketsueki
blood group: *my blood group is...*
  (watashi no) ketsueki gata wa ... dess
blood pressure: *I have high blood*
  pressure watashi wa kōketsu-atsu dess
blue *(n)* ao
  (adj) aoi
to board *(plane, train)* noru
boarding pass tōjōken
boat bōto
  (ship) fune
boiled rice gohan
bone hone
bonito katsuo
book *(reading)* hon
to book yoyak suru
  I'd like to book a table tēburu o yoyak
  shtai dess
  I'd like to book a flight to... ...yuki no bin
  o yoyak shtai dess
booking yoyak
booking office kipp uriba

boots būtsu
  (rubber) nagagutsu
to be born: *I was born in Scotland*
  Skottorando de umaremashta
to borrow: *can I borrow...?* ...o karite
  ī dess ka?
botanical gardens shokubutsu-en
both ryōhō no
  both A and B A to B no ryōhō
bottle bin ; botoru
bottle opener sen-nuki
bowl bōru ; wan
box hako
boy shōnen
boyfriend bōifrendo
bra brajā
bracelet bresretto ; udewa
brake fluid burēki eki
brake pads burēki ban
brakes burēki
  the brakes don't work burēki ga
  kikimasen
  please check the brakes burēki o chekku
  shte kudasai
branch *(bank)* shiten
  (company) shisha
  (of tree) eda
brandy burandē
bread pan
  sliced bread suraisu breddo ; kitta pan
  white bread shiro-pan
  wholemeal bread komugi haiga iri pan
to break kowasu
  we've broken down koshō shimashta
breakfast chōshoku ; asa-gohan
breast *(chicken)* mune-niku
to breathe: *I can't breathe* iki ga
  dekimasen
bride oyome ; shinpu

Cat

猫

Centre

中

Chair

椅子

Chemist

薬局

Child

子供

Chopsticks

箸

bridegroom grūm ; shinrō
bridge (game) brijji
(river, road, etc) hashi
briefcase kaban
to bring (thing) motte kuru
(person) tsurete kuru
would you like me to bring anything?
nani ka motte ikimashō ka?
please bring it to my room (watashi no)
heya ni motte-kite kudasai
Britain Igiriss ; Eikoku
British (adj) Eikoku-no
(person) Eikoku-jin
brochure panfretto
do you have any brochures?
panfretto wa arimass ka?
broken: *this is broken* kore wa kowarete
imass
brothers kyodai
older brother (own) ani
(somebody else's) o-nī-san
younger brother (own) otōto
(somebody else's) otōto-san
brown (n) cha-iro
(adj) cha-iro-no
Buddha hotoke
Buddhism bukkyō
Buddhist temple (o-)tera
building tatemono ; biru
bulb (light) denkyū
bullet train Shinkansen
bureau de change ryōgae-sho
burn: *it's burnt* (food) kogete imass
bus bass
business bijiness ; shigoto
business card meishi
business trip shu'chō
bus station bass ha'chakujo
bus stop bass tei

bus tour: *is there a bus tour?* bass tsuā
wa arimass ka?
busy isogashī
are you busy? isogashī dess ka
the line's busy (phone) hanashi chū dess
butcher's nikuya
butter batā
button botan
to buy kau
where can I buy...? doko de ... o kau
koto ga dekimass ka?
by: *by taxi* takshī de
by car kuruma de
by train densha de
by plane hikōki de
by bus bass de

C

cab *(taxi)* takshī
cabaret kyabarē
cabbage kyabets
cabin *(on ship)* kyabin
cable car kēburukā
caddy *(golf)* kyadī
café kissaten
cake *(western style)* kēki
cake shop kēkiya
calculator keisanki
to call *(phone)* ...ni denwa o kakeru
call *(phone call)* denwa
long-distance call chōkyori denwa
calm *(person)* ochitsuita
(weather) odayaka na tenki
camcorder bideo kamera
camera kamera
camera bag kamera bagu
camera shop kamera ya
camping kyanpu

City

市

Clock

時計

Closed

閉

132

Clothes

服

Comb

櫛

Cotton

木綿

can we go camping? kyanpu ni iku koto wa dekimass ka?
can *(n)* kan
can: *can I...?* ...dekimass ka?
can *(may)*: *may I...?* ...shtemo ī dess ka?
Canada Kanada
Canadian *(adj)* Kanada-no
  (person) Kanada-jin
to cancel: *I'd like to cancel my booking* yoyaku o torikeshtai dess
cancellation *(of flight)* kekkō
  (of train) unkyū
cancelled torikesareta
cancer gan
candle rōsok
canned kanzume
can opener kankiri
capital *(city)* shuto
  (money) shikin
captain *(ship)* senchō
  (plane) kyaputen
car kuruma ; jidōsha
car accessories kuruma yōhin
caravan kyaraban ; kyanping kā
carburettor kyaburetā
card *(business)* meishi
  (playing) toranpu
  (greetings) kādo
cardboard box danbōru-bako
cardphone kādo yō denwa
careful: *be careful!* ki o tskete!
  I will be very careful yoku ki o tskemas
careless: *how careless of me!* nante fuchūi nan deshō!
car hire rentakā sābiss
car keys kuruma no kagi
carp koi
car park chūshajō
carpet jūtan ; kāpetto

carriage *(train)* kyakusha
carrier bag kaimonobukuro
carrot ninjin
to carry hakobu
carsick: I get carsick kuruma ni yoimass
carwash sensha
case *(suitcase)* sūtskēsu ; ryokōkaban
cash *(n)* genkin
   we only take cash genkin barai nomi
   dess
cash dispenser ATM
   can I use this cash dispenser? kono ATM
   o tsukattemo ī dess ka?
cash desk (o-)kaikei
cash machine ATM
casino kajino
cassette kasetto
cassette player kasetto pureiyā
castle shiro
cat neko
to catch *(hold of)* tsukamu
to catch a cold kaze o hiku
cathedral dai-seidō
catholic katorikk kyōto
cauliflower karifurawā
cave dōkutsu
CD shīdī
CD player shīdī puraier
celery serori
cellphone keitai denwa
cemetery bochi
centigrade sesshi
centimetre senchimētoru
central chūshin-no
central heating danbō
centre chūshin ; chūō
century seiki
   21ˢᵗ century niju-isseiki

Country

国

Day

日

December

十
二
月

134

Departure

出発

Dinner

夕食

Disabled
people

障
害
者

ceramics tōki
cereal *(breakfast)* shiriāru
certain: *are you certain?* hontō dess ka?
certainly *(truth)* tashika-ni
certainly! *(I will do that)* yorokonde!
certificate shōmeishō
chain *(jewellery)* kusari
chainstore chēn-ten
chair isu
chambermaid jochū
champagne shanpen
chalet bessō
change *(money)* kozeni
  do you have any change? kozeni wa arimass ka?
to change: *where can I change some money?* doko de ryōgae (ga) dekimass ka?
  do I need to change trains? densha o norikaeru hitsuyō ga arimass ka?
changing room kōi-shits
charge *(fee)* tesū-ryō
  is there any charge? tesū-ryō wa kakarimass ka?
  free of charge tesū-ryō nashi
cheaper: *do you have anything cheaper?* motto yasui mono wa arimass ka?
to check chekk suru ; shiraberu
  can you check this for me? kore o chekk shte kudasai?
to check in: *where do I check in?* doko de chekk-in suru no dess ka?
check-in desk *(hotel)* furonto
to check out: *when should I check out by?* chekk-auto wa nan-ji made dess ka?
cheers! kanpai!
cheese chīzu
chef shefu
chemist *(scientist)* kagaku-sha

135

chemist's *(shop)* kusuriya ; yakkyok
cheque chekk ; kogitte
  do you accept cheques? kogitte wa
  tsukaemass ka?
cherry sakuranbo
cherry blossom sakura
chest *(of body)* mune
chestnuts kuri
chewing gum chūin-gamu
chicken *(bird)* niwatori
  (meat) toriniku
  (grilled) yaki-tori
chickenpox mizubōsō
children kodomotachi
  do you have any children? o-kosan
  wa imass ka?
  I don't have any children kodomo
  wa imasen
child seat chairudo shīto
chilli tōgarashi
china *(n)* setomono
China Chūgoku
Chinese *(adj)* Chūgoku-no
  (person) Chūgoku-jin
  (language) Chūgoku-go
chips *(french fries)* furaido poteto
chocolate(s) chokorēto
to choose: *I don't know what to choose*
  dore ni sureba yoi no ka wakarimasen
  you choose for me kawari ni erande
  kudasai
chopsticks (o-)hashi
Christian name senrei-mei
Christmas kurissmasu
Christmas Eve kurissmasu-ību
church kyōkai
  is there a Protestant/Catholic church?
  purotesutanto/katorikk kyōkai wa
  arimass ka?

Doctor

医者

Dog

犬

Door

戸

Down/under

下

East

東

Emergency exit

非

常

口

cigar hamaki
cigarette tabako
cigarette lighter raitā
 do you have a light? hi wa arimass ka?
cinema *(place)* eigakan
city machi ; tokai
city centre machi no chūshin
 how do I get to the city centre? machi
 no chūshin ewa dō ikeba ī dess ka?
claim *(n)* yōkyū
 to claim for yōkyū suru
class *(in school)* kumi ; kurasu
 business class bijiness kurass
 economy class ekonomī kurass
 first class fāsto kurass
 second class sekando kurass
classical music kurashikku ongaku
clean *(adj)* kirei-na
to clean *(house)* sōji suru
 can you clean this for me? kore o kirei
 ni dekimass ka?
 it is not clean kirei de wa arimasen
cleaner *(person)* seisō gyōsha
clerk ten-in
clever kashikoi
climate kikō ; fūdo
climbing *(mountains)* yama nobori
climbing boots tozan gutsu
cling film saran rapp
clinic kurinikku ; shinryōjo
cloakroom kurōku ; tenimots azukari-sho
 where's the cloakroom? kurōku wa doko
 dess ka?
clock tokei
to close: *when do you close?* itsu
 shimarimass ka?
close by chikaku
closed *(shops)* heiten
cloth nuno

137

clothes fuku

cloudy kumotte-iru

club kurabu
  are you a member of a club? kurabu no kai-in dess ka?

clutch *(car)* kuratchi

coach *(bus)* bass
  (of train) kyakusha
  coach station bass noriba

coal sekitan

coast kaigan

coat kōto ; uwagi

coat hanger hangā
  I need more coat hangers motto hangā ga irimass

Coca Cola® kokakōra

cockroach gokiburi

coffee kōhī
  black coffee burakku kōhī
  white coffee miruku kōhī
  decaffeinated coffee kafein muki no kōhī
  cappuccino kapuchino

cognac konyakk

coin koin ; -dama
  ten-yen coin ju-en-dama

cold: *it's cold (room)* samui dess
  I'm cold watashi wa samui dess
  it's cold (food) tsumetai dess

cold: *I have a cold* kaze o hīte imass

colleague dōryō

to collect: *can you collect my luggage?* (watashi no) nimots o tori ni kite itadakemass ka?
  when will it be collected? itsu tori ni kite itadakemass ka?

collect call korekuto kōru ; ryōkin jushin-nin barai

Entrance

入口

Exit

出口

February

二月

college *(university)* **daigaku**
  (junior college) **tandai**
colour iro
colourfast: is it colourfast? iro ga
  kawarimasen ka?
colour film *(for camera)* kārā firumu
comb kushi
to come kuru
  when can you come? itsu nara tsugō
  ga yoi dess ka?
  come in! dōzo!
comedy komedī
comfortable: *this is very comfortable*
  totemo kimochi ga ī dess
comics *(publications)* manga
commercial *(on TV)* komāsharu ; CM
common *(usual)* futsū-no
communism kyōsan shugi
compact disc konpakuto disuku ; shīdī
company *(firm)* kaisha
company director shacho ; jōmu
compartment *(train)* koshits
competition kyōsō
competitive price kyōsō-kakaku
complaint: I have a complaint kujō ga
  arimass
to complete kansei suru
complicated: *it's very complicated* taihen
  fukuzats dess
composer sakkyoku-ka
compulsory: is it compulsory? sore wa
  dōshtemo hitsuyō dess ka?
computer konpyūta
computer game konpyūta gemu
computer programmer konpyūta
  puroguramā
concert konsāto
concert hall konsāto hōru
concussion noshintō ; gekidō

conditioner *(hair)* rinsu
condom kondōmu
conductor *(music)* shikisha
conference kaigi
conference centre kaigi jō
to confirm: *do I need to confirm?* kakunin suru hitsuyō ga arimass ka?
I want to confirm my booking yoyaku no kakunin o onegai shimass
congratulations omedetō gozaimass
to connect: *I'm trying to connect you* o-tsunagi shte imass
connection *(train, plane)* noritsugi *(electronic)* setsuzoku
constipated: *I'm constipated* benpi dess
consul ryōji
consulate ryōjikan
where is the British consulate? Igiriss ryōjikan wa doko dess ka?
contact lens cleaner kontakuto renzu kurīnā
contact lenses kontakuto renzu
continent tairik
contraceptive *(n)* hinin-yaku ; hinin-yōhin
controls *(car)* sōjūsōchi ; kontorōru
convenient benri na ; tsugō no ī
is it convenient for you? (anata ni totte) tsugō ga ī dess ka?
it isn't convenient for me (watashi ni totte) tsugō ga yoku arimasen
cook *(n)* kokku
(Japanese restaurants) itamae
to cook ryōri o suru
how do you cook this? dō yatte kore o ryōri shimass ka?
cooker rēnji
copy *(n)* kopī
can I make a copy? kopī o tottemo ī dess ka?

Food

食
べ
物

Forest

Friday

cork koruku
  (bottle) botoru no sen
corkscrew sen-nuki
corn tōmorokoshi
corner kado
correct: *is it correct?* tadashī dess ka?
corridor rōka
cost *(n)* kosuto
to cost: *how much does it cost?* ikura kakarimass ka?
cotton wata
cotton wool kiwata
cough *(n)* seki
to count kazoeru
counter *(in shop, etc)* kauntā
country *(not town)* inaka
  (state) kuni
couple *(people)* kappuru ; futarizure
courgettes zukkīni
courier kūriā
  I want to send this by courier kūria de kore o okuritai dess
course *(study)* kōsu
  (meal) kōsu menyū
  of course mochiron
court *(law)* hōtei
  (tennis) kōto
cousin itoko
crab kani
crafts kōgeihin
cramp keiren
crayfish zarigani
cream kurīmu
credit shinyo
credit card krejitto kādo
cricket *(game)* kuriketto
crisps poteto chippus
cross *(n)* jūji

crossing *(ferry)*: *when is the next crossing?* tsugi no ferī wa itsu dess ka?

crossroads jūjiro

crowd hitogomi

crown *(on tooth)* ha ni kabuseru mono ; shikan

cruise *(n)* funatabi

to cry *(weep)* naku

cucumber kyūri

cup kappu

cupboard todana

cure *(healing)* naori
   (remedy) chiryōhō

current *(electricity)* denryū

curtains kāten

cushion kusshon

customs zeikan

customs declaration zeikan shinkoku

cut *(n)* kirikizu

to cut kiru

cute kawairashī

cutlery hamono-rui

cybercafé intānet kafe

cycling saikuringu

D

daily *(each day)* mainichi-no

damage *(n)* higai

dance *(n)* odori

to dance dansu o suru ; odoru

dangerous abunai ; kiken

dark *(colour)* kurai

date *(day of month)* hizuke
   (formal appointment) hidori

date of birth seinen-gappi

daughter *(own)* musume
   (somebody else's) musume-san ; o-jō-san

day hi ; nichi
   per day ichi nichi de
   every day mai nichi

Garden

庭

Gate

門

Gram

グラム

deaf mimi no kikoenai
dear *(expensive)* kōka-na
decaffeinated kafein nuki-no
December jū-ni-gats
deep fukai
degree *(temperature)* do
  (university) gakui
delay: *how long is the delay?* donokurai
  okuremass ka?
to be delayed *(plane, train, etc)* okureru
dentist ha-isha
dentures ireba
deodorant bōshūzai ; deodoranto
department store depāto ; hyakkaten
departure shuppats
departure lounge shuppats raunji
deposit *(to pay)* hoshōkin
dessert dezāto
destination mokuteki-chi
detergent senzai
diabetic tōnyōbyō-no
to dial daiyaru shimass
dialling code kyokuban
diarrhoea geri
diary nikki
dictionary jisho
diet daietto ; shokuji ryōhō
different chigau ; kotonaru
digital camera dejitaru kamera
digital radio dejitaru rajio
dining room shokudō ; dainingu rūmu
dinner yūshoku ; dinā
direct *(train, etc)* chokutsū
direction hōkō
directory jūsho-shimei-roku
dirty kitanai
disabled shōgai no aru
disco disuko

discount waribiki
dish (o-)sara
disinfectant shōdoku-yaku
disk disuku
disposable tsukaisute-no
district chihō
divorce (n) rikon
divorced rikonshta
dizzy: *to feel dizzy* memai ga suru
to do shimass
doctor isha ; doktā
document bunsho
dog inu
doll ningyō
dollar doru
door to ; doā
double nijū-no
   (quantity) nibai-no
double bed daburu beddo
double room daburu rūmu ; futari beya
download daunrōdo suru
draught *(air)* sukima-kaze
   (draught beer) nama bīru
to draw *(picture)* e o kaku
dress (n) doress ; yōfuku
dressing *(medical)* hōtai
   (salad) doreshingu
drink nomimono
to drink nomimas
to drive unten suru ; doraibu suru
driver *(of car)* untenshu
driving licence unten-menkyoshō
drug *(medical)* kusuri ; yakuhin
to dry *(clothes, etc)* kawakasu
dry-cleaner's dorai-kurīningu-ya
duck ahiru
duty-free menzei-no
duvet kakebuton

Headache

頭痛

Hiroshima

広島

Hokkaido

北
海
道

Honshu

本州

Hospital

病院

Hot spring

温泉

E

each sorezore-no
ear mimi
earache mimi no itami
early hayaku
earplugs mimi sen
earrings iyaringu
earthquake jishin
east higashi
Easter īsutā
to eat taberu
  I don't eat meat watashi wa nikk
  o tabemasen
  I don't eat fish watashi wa sakana
  o tabemasen
  I don't eat eggs watashi wa tamago
  o tabemasen
edible shokuyō-no
eel unagi
egg tamago
  fried egg medama-yaki
  hard-boiled egg kata yude tamago
  scrambled eggs iri tamago
eggplant nasu
elastic wa-gomu
electrician denkiya
electricity denki ; denryoku
electric razor denki-kamisor
elevator erebētā
e-mail denshi meru ; ē meru
  to send an e-mail ē meru o okuru
  this is my e-mail address watāshi no
  ēmeru adoress dess
embassy taishikan
emergency kinkyū
emergency exit hijōguchi
emperor tennō
empty kara

engaged (couple) kon-yaku shte-iru
(phone) hanashi-chū
(toilet) shiyō-chū
England Igiriss
English (adj) Igiriss-no
(person) Igiriss-jin
(language) Eigo
enough: *that's enough* (food etc) mō
kekkō dess
that's enough! (stop!) yamenasai!
enquiry desk uketsuke
to enter (a place) hairu
entrance iriguchi
entrance fee nyūjō-ryō
envelope fūtō
epileptic tenkan-no
epileptic fit tenkan sei keiren
equipment setsubi
escalator esukarētā
euro yūro
Europe yōroppa
evening yoru ; ban
  in the evening yoru ni
evening meal yūshoku
example: *for example* tatoeba
excellent subarashī
excess baggage chōka te-nimots
exchange rate kawase rēto
excursion ensok
excuse me! sumimasen!
exhaust pipe haikikan
exhibition tenjikai
exit deguchi
expensive kōka-na
exports yushutsu-hin
express train kyūkō
extension (electrical) enchō kōdo
(phone) naisen

In

入

Information

案内

Insect

昆虫

146

extra *(additional)* **yobun-no**
eye **me**
eye drops **megusuri**

F

fabric **kiji**
factory **kōjō**
to faint **kizetsu suru**
fair *(just)* **kōhei-na**
  (funfair) **yūenchi**
false teeth **ireba**
family **kazoku**
fan *(hand-held)* **uchiwa ; sensu**
  (electric) **senpūki**
fanbelt **fanberuto**
far **tōi**
fare *(bus, etc)* **ryōkin**
Far East **Kyokutō**
farm **nōka**
fast **hayai**
fat *(person)* **futotta**
father *(own)* **chichi**
  (somebody else's) **otō-san**
faulty *(machine, etc)* **kekkan no aru**
fax **fakks**
  my fax **watashi no fakkuso**
  fax number **fakks bangō**
to fax **fakks o okuru**
February **ni-gats**
fee **ryōkin**
female *(adj)* **onna-no**
ferry **ferī**
festival **matsuri**
to fetch **totte kuru**
few: *a few* **ni san no**
fiancé(e) **fianse ; kon-yakusha**
file *(computer, document)* **fairu**
to fill *(up)* **mitasu**
  fill it up! **ippai ni shte!**

filling *(tooth)* tsumemono
film *(for camera)* firumu
  (cinema) eiga
to find mitsukeru
  I can't find... ...mitsukari masen
fine *(penalty)* bakkin
finger yubi
fire: *house fire* kaji ; kasai
  camp fire takibi
fire alarm kasai-hōchi-ki
fire brigade shōbōtai
fire escape hijōkaídan
fire extinguisher shōkakki
fireworks hanabi
firm *(company)* kaisha
first saisho-no
first aid okyū-teate
first aid kit kyūkyūbako
first class fāsuto kurass
first floor *(above ground floor)* nikai
first name namae
fish *(n)* sakana
to fit: *it doesn't fit* aimasen
fitting room shichaku shits
to fix: *can you fix it?* naose mass ka?
flat *(apartment)* apāto
  (battery) batterī ga agaru
flat tyre panku
flavour aji
floor *(of building)* -kai
  first floor ikkai
  second floor ni-kai
  (of room) yuka
flower hana
flu infuruenza
fly *(insect)* hae
to fly tobu
food tabemono
food poisoning shokuchū-doku

July

七月

June

六月

Kagoshima

鹿
児
島

148

foot ashi
football (soccer) sakkā
for (in exchange for) ...no kawari ni
foreign gaikoku-no
forest mori
fork (cutlery) fōku
fortnight nishūkan
fountain izumi ; funsui
foyer robī
fracture (of bone) kossets
fragrance kaori
frame (picture) gaku
free (not occupied) aiteiru
  (costing nothing) muryō-no
  (not constrained) jiyū (na)
fresh (food) shinsen
Friday kin-yōbi
fridge reizōko
fried food agemono
friend tomodachi
fruit kudamono
fruit juice furūts jūs
fuel nenryō
fuel gauge nenryō kei
full ippai
  I'm full onaka ga ippai dess
full board sanshok-tsuki no shukuhak
funfair yūenchi
funny (amusing) omoshiroi
  (strange) okashī ; kawatta
fuse hyūzu
fuse box hyūzu bokksu

G

gallery gyararī ; garō
game gēmu
garage garēji
garden niwa

garlic nin-niku
gastritis ichōen ; i-en
gate mon
  (airport) gēto
gay *(bright)* hanayaka-na
  (homosexual) gei
gears gīya
  (cogs) haguruma
generous kandai-na
gentleman shinshi
gents *(toilet)* dansei-yō toire
genuine honmono
to get *(obtain)* eru
  (to fetch thing) motte kuru
  (to fetch person, animal) tsurete kuru
to get in *(car)* noru
to get off *(bus, etc)* oriru
gift okurimono
gift shop gifuto shoppu
ginger shōga
girl shōjo
  (polite) ojō-san
girlfriend kanojo ; gārufurendo
to give ageru
to give back kaesu ; modosu
glass guras
glasses *(spectacles)* megane
gloves tebukuro
glue nori
to go iku
to go back modoru
to go in hairu
gold kin
golf goruf
golf ball goruf bōru
golf club goruf kurab
golf course goruf kōs
good yoi
good afternoon kon-nichi wa
goodbye sayonara

Left

左

Letter

Library

good evening konban wa
good morning o-hayō gozaimass
good night oyasumi nasai
to go out dekakeru
granddaughter magomusume
grandfather *(own)* sofu
  (somebody else's) ojī-san
grandmother *(own)* sobo
  (somebody else's) obā-san
grandson magomusuko
grapefruit gurēpufurūtsu
grapes budō
great *(large)* ōkī
green *(n)* midori
  (adj) midori-no
greengrocer yaoya
grey *(n)* hai-iro ; gurei
  (adj) hai-iro-no ; gurei-no
grilled yaita ; yaki-
grocer's shokuryōhin-ten
ground floor ikkai
group *(people)* gurūpu ; kumi
guarantee *(n)* hoshō
guarantor hoshonin
guard *(on train)* shashō
guest *(to house)* okyakusama
guest house gesuto hausu
guide *(n)* gaido ; an-nai
to guide gaido o suru ; an-nai o suru
guidebook gaidobukk
guided tour gaido-tsuki tsuā

H

hair kami ; kami-noke
hairbrush heāburashi
haircut sanpats ; heākatto
hairdresser's *(for men)* tokoya
  (for women) biyōin

hair dryer heādoraiyā
hair gel heā no jeru
hairspray heāsuprē
half: *a half bottle of...* ...no shōbin
half-price hangaku-no
hall *(for concerts, etc)* hōru ; kan
ham hamu
handbag handobaggu
handicapped shintaishōgai no aru
  (person) shogaisha
handkerchief hankachi
handle handoru ; tesuri
hand luggage tenimots
hand-made tezukuri-no
to happen okoru
  what happened? dō shimashta ka?
hard *(firm)* katai
  (difficult) muzukashī
hat bōshi
hay fever kafunshō
head atama
headache zutsū
headlights hedoraito
head office honsha
headphones heddohōn
hearing aid hochōki
heart *(emotional)* kokoro
  (organ) shinzō
heart attack shinzōmahi
to heat up *(food)* atatameru
heater hītā
heavy *(weight)* omoi
hello kon-nichi wa
  (on phone) moshi moshi
to help tetsudau
  help! taskete!
  it can't be helped shikata ga nai
herb hābu ; yakusō
here koko (ni)

May
五月

Medicine
薬

Milk
牛乳

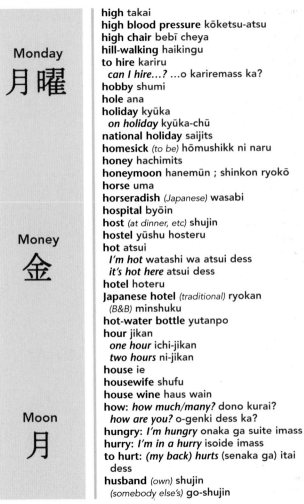

Monday

月曜

high takai
high blood pressure kōketsu-atsu
high chair bebī cheya
hill-walking haikingu
to hire kariru
  can I hire...? ...o kariremass ka?
hobby shumi
hole ana
holiday kyūka
  on holiday kyūka-chū
national holiday saijits
homesick *(to be)* hōmushikk ni naru
honey hachimits
honeymoon hanemūn ; shinkon ryokō
horse uma
horseradish *(Japanese)* wasabi
hospital byōin
host *(at dinner, etc)* shujin
hostel yūshu hosteru
hot atsui
  I'm hot watashi wa atsui dess
  it's hot here atsui dess

Money

金

hotel hoteru
Japanese hotel *(traditional)* ryokan
  (B&B) minshuku
hot-water bottle yutanpo
hour jikan
  one hour ichi-jikan
  two hours ni-jikan
house ie
housewife shufu
house wine haus wain
how: *how much/many?* dono kurai?
  how are you? o-genki dess ka?
hungry: *I'm hungry* onaka ga suite imass
hurry: *I'm in a hurry* isoide imass
to hurt: *(my back) hurts* (senaka ga) itai
  dess
husband *(own)* shujin
  (somebody else's) go-shujin

Moon

月

I

I watashi
  (polite) watakushi
ice kōri ; aisu
ice cream aisukurīmu
identity card mibunshōmeisho
ignition key kākī
ill: *...is ill* ...wa byōki dess
illegal fuhō-no ; īho-no
immediately sugu-ni
important taisets (na)
imports yunyū
indigestion shōka furyō
indoors okunai de
inflammation enshō
information jōhō
information office annai-sho
inhaler kokyūki
injection chūsha
to be injured kega o suru
inquiry desk annai sho
insect konchū
insect repellent mushi-yoke
inside ...no naka ni
  inside the car kuruma no naka ni
instant coffee instanto kōhī
instructions *(for use)* toriatsukai setsumei
instructor shidōsha ; sensei
insulin inshurin
insurance hoken
insurance certificate hokenshō
international kokusaiteki (na)
Internet intā netto
Internet café intānetto kafe
interpreter tsūyakusha
interval *(theatre)* kyūkei

Morning

朝

Mountain

山

Museum

博
物
館

Nagasaki

長崎

Nagoya

名
古
屋

Nara

奈良

to introduce *(a person)* shōkai suru
invitation shōtai
to invite shōtai suru
invoice okurijō ; seikyūsho
Ireland Airurando
Irish *(adj)* Airurando-no
  (person) Airurando-jin
iron *(for clothes)* airon
  (metal) tets
ironmonger's kanamono-ya
island shima
itemized bill seikyū meisaisho

J

jack *(for car)* jakki
jacket jakketto
jam *(food)* jamu
  traffic jam kōtsu jūtai
  jammed *(with people)* komiatta
  (paper in copier) tsumatta
January ichi-gats
Japan Nihon ; Nippon
Japanese *(language)* Nihongo
  (adj) Nihon-no
  (person) Nihon-jin
jeweller's hōseki-ten
jewellery hōseki-rui
job shigoto
to jog jogingu o suru
journey ryokō
juice *(fruit)* jūsu
  (of something) shiru ; eki
July shichi-gats
Jump leads būstā-kēburu
junction *(roads)* kōsaten
June roku-gats
just: *just two* futats dake
  I've just arrived tsuita bakari dess

K

key *(for lock)* kagi
kidneys *(food)* ingenmame
kilo kiro
kilometre kiromētā
kind *(n)* shurui
  (adj) shinsets-na
king kokuō ; kingu
kitchen daidokoro
knickers pantī
knife naifu
  (Japanese) hōchō
to knock down *(car)* (kuruma ga) haneru
knot musubime ; kobu
to know *(facts)* shiru
  I don't know Tokyo watashi wa Tokyo
  o shirimasen
Korea Kankoku

L

label raberu ; fuda
lace rēsu
shoe lace kutsu-himo
ladies *(toilet)* fujin-yō toire
lager ragā bīru
lake mizu-umi
lamb *(meat)* ramu
land *(n)* tochi
lane *(narrow road)* komichi
  (on motorway) shasen
language gengo ; kotoba
large ōkī
late osoi
  the train is late densha ga okurete
  imass
launderette koin randorī
laundry service kurīningu-ya
lavatory senmenjo

Night

夜

Niigata

新潟

North

北

156

No-smoking

禁煙

November

十
一
月

Number

番号

lawyer bengoshi
leader *(of group)* rīdā
leaflet chirashi
leak *(n)* *(of gas, liquid)* more
to learn manabu
leather kawa
to leave shuppats suru ; saru
  (leave behind) oite iku
left: *on/to the left* hidari ni
left luggage *(office)* tenimots ichiji
  azukari-sho
leg ashi
lemon remon
lens renzu
lesson ressun ; jigyō
letter *(mail)* tegami
letterbox yūbin-uke
lettuce retasu
library toshokan
licence menkyosho ; raisensu
to lie down yoko ni naru ; nekorobu
lifebelt kyūmeigu
life boat kyūmei-bōto
life guard mihari ; kyūjo-in
life jacket raifu jakketo
lift *(elevator)* erebētā
light: *do you have a light?* hi wa
  arimass ka?
light bulb denkyū
lighter raitā
lightning inazuma
to like: konomu ; suki
  I like coffee kōhī ga suki dess
  I'd like... ...ga hoshii dess
like this kono yō ni ; kō iu fū ni
lime raimu
line *(railway)* sen
  (drawn) rain
lip-reading shiwahō ; dokushin-juts

lipsalve kuchibiru yō nankō
list hyō ; risuto
to listen to... ...o kiku
litre rittoru
little: *a little* sukoshi
to live (in a place) sumu ; kurasu
   I live in London Rondon ni sunde imass
   (to be alive) ikiru
   (he) is alive (kare wa) ikitteimass
liver rebā
living room ima
lobster robstā
local (wine, speciality) jimoto-no
lock (on door, box) kagi ; rokk
to lock kagi o kakeru
locker rokkā
long nagai
   for a long time nagai aida
to look for sagasu
loose (not fastened) yurui
to lose: *I've lost...* ...o naku shimashta
lost (object) nakushta
lost-property office ishitsubuts
   toriatsukaijo
lot: *a lot* takusan
lotion rōshon
loud (person) koe no ōkī
   (surroundings) yakamashī ; sōzōshī
lounge (in hotel) raunji
love (n) ai
   I love swimming suiei ga daiski dess
low-alcohol tei alkōru no
luggage tenimots
luggage allowance tenimots seigen
luggage rack (in car, train) amidana
luggage trolley nimots tororī ; daisha
lunch hiru gohan ; ranchi
luxury zeitaku

Occupied

使
用
中

October

十月

Old people

老人

158

Open

開

Osaka

大阪

Otaru

小樽

M

machine kikai
magazine zasshi
maid jochū ; meido
  (polite) jochū-san ; meido-san
mail *(n)* yūbin
  e-mail ē meiru
  by mail yūbin de
mains *(electric)* honkan
to make tsukuru
make-up (o-)keshō
man *(general)* hito
  (male) otoko
manager sekininsha ; manējā
many takusan-no
map chizu
marathon marason
March san-gats
market ichiba ; māketto
marmalade māmarēdo
to get/be married kekkon suru
  (they/we are) a married couple fūfu dess
martial arts budō
mask kamen ; masku
mass *(in church)* misa
match *(game)* shiai
matches matchi
material *(fabric)* kiji
to matter: it doesn't matter kamaimasen
  what's the matter? dō shimashta ka?
mattress mattoresu
May go-gats
meal shoku-ji
to mean: what does this mean? kore wa
  dō iu imi dess ka?
meat (o-)nik
mechanic kikaikō ; mekkanik
medical insurance iryō-hoken

medicine kusuri
medieval chūsei-no
to meet au
let's meet again mata aimashō
meeting mītingu ; kaigi
member *(of club, etc)* kai-in ; menbā
menu menyū
message dengon ; messeiji
metre mētā
microwave chin
to microwave chin suru
midday ohiru
  at midday ohiru ni
middle-aged chūnen-no
midnight mayonaka
migraine henzutsū
mile mairu
milk miruku ; gyūnyū
  semi-skimmed teishibō gyūnyū
  soya milk tōnyū
millimetre mirimētoru
million *(n)* hyaku-man
  (adj) hyaku-man-no
mineral water mineraru uōtā
minibar mini bā
minute fun
  one minute ippun
  two minutes nifun
mirror kagami
to miss *(train, etc)* norisokonau
missing *(person)* yukuefumei-no
mistake *(n)* machigai
misunderstanding: *there must be a misunderstanding* gokai ni chigai arimasen
mobile phone keitai denwa
modem mōdemu
monastery shūdōin
Monday getsu-yōbi

Out

出

Out of order

故障

Overground

地上

Park

公園

Pear

梨

Person

人

money (o-)kane
I have no money watashi wa okane ga arimasen
month tsuki
moon tsuki
more: *more wine please* motto wain o kudasai
no more thank you mo kekkō dess
morning asa
in the morning gozenchū ni
this morning kesa
mosquito ka
mother *(own)* haha
(somebody else's) okā-san
motor mōtā ; hatsudōki
motorbike ōtobai ; baik
motorboat mōtā bōto
motorway kōsoku dōro
mountain yama
mountain bike maunten baik
mountain rescue sangaku kyūjotai
mouse *(animal)* nezumi
(computer) mausu
mouth kuchi
Mr... ...-shi ; ...-san
Mrs... ...-san ; ...-fujin
Ms... ...-san
much: *there's too much* ōsugiru
mugged: *I've been mugged* dorobo ga hairimashta
museum hakubutsu-kan
mushroom masshurūmu
(Japanese) shītake ; matsutake
music ongaku
mussel murasaki igai ; mūru-gai

N

nail *(finger)* tsume
(metal) kugi
name namae

what's your name? o-namae wa nan dess ka?
nappy omutsu
narrow semai
nationality kokseki
nausea hakike
near chikaku ni
  near the bank ginkō no chikaku (ni)
necessary hitsuyō-na
neck kubi
necklace nekkuress
to need: *I need...* ...ga hitsuyō dess
needle hari
negative *(photograph)* nega
neighbour kinjo no hito
nephew oi
never *(adv)* kesshte ... masen
  I never drink wine kesshte wain o nomimasen
new atarashī
news nyūsu ; (o-)shirase
newspaper shinbun
New Year shin nen
New Zealand Nyū Jīrando
New Zealander *(person)* Nyū Jīrando-jin
next: *next week* raishū
  next year rainen
  the next train tsugi no densha
night yoru
  at night yoru (ni)
  last night sakuya ; yūbe
  tomorrow night ashta no yoru
nightclub naito kurabu
nightdress nemaki
no ī-e
  no thank you ī-e kekkō dess
noisy yakamashī ; urusai
non-alcoholic arukōru nuki-no
non-smoking kin-en
non-smoking compartment kinen sharyō

Platform

Police station

Post office

162

noodles men-rui ; udon ; soba ; ramen
noon ohiru
north kita
Northern Ireland Kita Airurando
note *(banknote)* shihei
  (letter) tsūtats ; memo
November jū-ichi-gats
now ima
nowadays konogoro
number *(of)* kazu
number *(1, 2, 3, etc)* sūji
numberplate *(on car)* nanbā pureito
nurse kangofu
nut *(peanut, etc)* nattsu ; konomi
  (for bolt) tome-neji

O

object *(thing)* mono
October jū-gats
octopus tako
of *(possessive)* ...no
  Queen of England Igiriss no jō-ō
  edge of the table tēburu no hashi
off *(light)* kieteiru
  (food) kusatteiru
office ofisu ; jimusho
often yoku
oil abura
oil filter oirufirutā
oil gauge oiru kei
ointment nankō
OK
  I'm OK, it's OK kekkō dess ; daijōbu
  dess
  OK, let's do that ō-kei ; sō shimashō
old: *how old are you?* nan sai dess ka?
olive orību
omelette omurets
on *(light)* tsuiteiru
  on the table tēburu no ue ni

one *(adj)* hitotsu-no
  (n) **ichi**
one-way ticket katamichi kippu
onion tamanegi
to open akeru
  the shop is open eigyō chu dess
  the door is open dōa ga aitteimass
  what time does it open? nanji ni
  akimass ka?
operation *(medical)* shujuts
opposite *(hand, side)* hantai-no
opposite *(meaning)* gyaku
optician megane-ya
orange *(adj)* orenji-iro-no
  (fruit) **orenji**
orange juice orenji jūsu
order: *out of order* koshō-chū
out *(light)* kieteiru
  he's out kare wa gaishuts-chū dess
outdoor *(pool, etc)* kogai-no
oven ōbun
overnight: *to spend one night* ippak suru
overnight train yakō densha
oysters kaki
ozone ozon

P

pacemaker pēsmēkā
Pacific Ocean taiheiyō
packet kozutsumi
painful itai
painkiller chintsūzai
painting e
oil painting abura-e
pair: *a pair of shoes* kutsu issok
palace kyūden
pants *(trousers)* zubon
  (men's underwear) **pantsu**
  (women's underwear) **panti**

Push

押

Rain

雨

Razor

剃刀

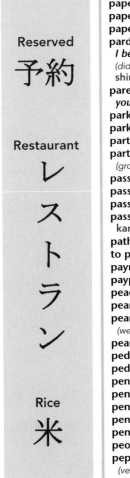

Reserved

予約

Restaurant

レ
ス
ト
ラ
ン

Rice

米

paper kami ; pēpā
paper handkerchief tisshu
paper towels kami taoru ; kitchen pepā
pardon? sumimasen
  I beg your pardon! sumimasen!
  (didn't hear/understand) mō ichido onegai
  shimass
parents ryōshin
  your parents go-ryōshin
park *(garden)* kōen
parking lot chūsha-jo ; pākingu
partner *(wife, husband)* haigūsha
party *(evening)* pātī
  (group) ikkō ; ichidan
pass *(permit)* kyokashō
passenger jōkyaku
passport paspōto
passport control shutsunyūkoku
  kanrisho
path komichi
to pay harau
payment shiharai
payphone kōshū denwa
peach momo
peanut pīnatts
pear *(Japanese)* nashi
  (western) yōnashi
pearl shinju
pedestrian *(n)* hokōsha
pedestrian crossing ōdanhodō
pen pen
pencil enpits
penicillin penishirin
penfriend penfurendo
pensioner nenkin-juryōsha
people hitobito
pepper *(spice)* koshō
  (vegetable) pīman
per: *per hour* ichijikan nitsuki

per week isshukan nitsuki
per person hitori nitsuki
per cent pāsento
performance pafōmansu
perfume kōsui
period *(menstruation)* seiri ; gekkei
permit *(authorisation)* kyokashō
persimmon kaki
person hito
personal organizer denshi techō
personal stereo keitai stereo ; uōkman
petrol gasorin
petrol station gasorin stando
petrol tank *(in car)* gasorin tank
pharmacy yakkyoku
phone *(n)* denwa
to phone denwa o kakeru
phone box denwa boks
phonecard terehon-kādo
phone number denwa-bangō
photocopy *(n)* kopī
to make a photocopy kopī o suru
photograph *(n)* shashin
to photograph shashin o toru
phrase book jukugo-shū
picnic pikunik
picture *(painting)* e ; kaiga
  (photo) shashin
pig buta
pill kusuri
  contraceptive pill piru
pillow makura
pineapple painappuru
plan *(of a building)* zumen
to plan kikaku suru
plane *(aircraft)* hikōki
plaster *(sticking plaster)* bando-eido
plastic bag pori-bukuro

Right
右

River
川

Road
道路

Ryokan

旅館

Sale

値
引
き

Sapporo

札幌

platform *(railway)* hōmu
play *(theatre)* geki
please dōzo
plug *(electrical)* puragu ; sashikomi
plug socket konsento
plum *(Japanese, green)* ume
  (western, purple) puram
plumber haikankō ; suidōya
p.m. *(after noon)* gogo
poisonous yūdoku-na
police keisats
policeman keisats kan
police station kōban
pool *(swimming)* pūru
pork buta-niku
porter *(hotel)* pōtā
portion *(of food)* ichinin-mae
postbox yūbin-uke
postcard e-hagaki ; postokādo
post office yūbin-kyok
potato jagaimo
pottery tōki-rui ; setomono
pound pondo
power cut teiden
power point konsento
prawn tenaga-ebi ; kuruma-ebi
pregnant ninshin shte iru
prescription shohōsen
present okurimono ; prezento
president *(of a company)* ...shachō
pretty kirei-na
price nedan
priest *(Buddhist)* sōryo
  (Catholic) shimpu
  (Protestant) bokushi
prime minister sōridaijin
prince ōji
princess ōjo

private kojin-no
prize shōhin
problem mondai
  there's a problem mondai ga arimass
programme *(TV, etc)* bangumi
  (computer) **puroguram**
promise: *it's a promise* yaksok dess
to pronounce: *how is it pronounced?*
  dono yō ni hatsuon shimass ka?
Protestant shinkyōto
prune purūn
public holiday saijits
public toilet koshū benjo
to pull hiku
puncture panku
puppet ayatsuri ningyō
pure *(gold, silver, etc)* junsui-na
purse saifu
push osu
pushchair buggi/bebīka

Q

qualification shikaku
quality hinshits
queen jō-ō
question *(n)* shitsumon
queue retsu
to queue retsu o tsukuru
quickly hayaku
quiet *(place)* shizuka-na
quilt kiruto

R

rabies kyōkenbyō
race *(sport)* kyōsō ; rēsu
  (people) jinshu
radio rajio
radish *(small, red)* radish ; hatsuka daikon
  (Japanese) daikon

Saturday

土曜

School

学校

Sea

海

railway station eki
rain ame
  it's raining ame ga futte imass
rare *(unique)* mare-na
  (steak) **rea-no** ; namayake-no
rash *(skin)* hasshin
rate *(of exchange)* rēto
raw nama-no
razor kamisori
razor blades kamisori no ha
ready junbi ga dekita
receipt ryōshusho ; reshīto
reception *(desk)* uketsuke
receptionist uketsukegakari
to recharge *(battery)* saijūden suru
recipe reshipī ; chōrihō
to recommend: *what do you recommend?*
  nani ga osusume dess ka?

record *(music, etc)* rekōdo
red *(n)* aka
  (adj) akai
reduction *(for student, etc)* waribiki
refreshments keishoku
refund: *I'd like a refund* henkin shte
  kudasai
region chi'iki ; chihō
to reimburse hensai suru
relative *(family member)* shinseki
relatively *(comparitively)* hikakuteki
reliable *(person)* shinrai dekiru
religion shūkyō
to remember omoidasu

to rent kariru
rent *(for house, flat)* yachin
to repair shūri suru ; naosu
repeat: *would you repeat that, please?*
  mō ichidō itte kudasai
reservation yoyaku
reserved yoyaku-shta

169

reserved seat shitei-seki
resort *(seaside)* rizōto
rest *(relaxation)* kyūsoku
to rest kyūsoku suru
restaurant restoran
restaurant car shokudōsha
restroom toire
retired intai shta ; taishoku shta
to return *(to go back)* kaeru ; modoru
  (to give back) kaesu
  (to return a purchase) henpin suru
return ticket ofuku-ken
reverse-charge call *(collect call)* korekuto
  kōru
rheumatism ryūmachi
rice okome
  (cooked) gohan
rich *(food)* nōkō-na
  (person) yūfuku-na
riding jōba
  to go riding jōba ni iku
right *(correct)* tadashī
  on/to the right migi ni
ring *(for finger)* yubiwa
river kawa
road michi ; dōro
road map dōro chizu
road sign dōro hyōshiki
to roast, bake or grill yaku
room *(in house, hotel)* heya
  (space) basho
  it takes up room basho o torimass
room service rūmu sābisu
rotten *(meat, fruit)* kusatta
rounabout *(in road)* rōtarī
roundabout route mawari-michi
route rūto
row *(theatre, etc)* retsu
royal kokuō-no ; ōshitsu-no

Shimonoseki

下関

Shizuoka

静岡

Shoes

靴

rubbish gomi
(nonsense) tawagoto
rucksack ryukksak
rush hour rasshu

S

safe *(adj)* anzen-na
safety belt anzenberuto
safety pin anzen pin
sailing *(sport)* seiringu
salad sarada
salary sararī ; kyūryō
sale *(in shops)* sēru
salesman seirusuman *(in store)* ten-in
salmon sake
salt shio
sandals sandaru
sandwich sandoitchi
sanitary towel seiriyō napukin
sardine iwashi
satellite TV eisei terebi
Saturday do-yōbi
sauce sōsu
to save *(life)* sukuu
(money) takuwaeru ; chokin suru
to say iu
scales *(for weighing)* hakari
scenery keshiki
school gakkō
scissors hasami
Scotland Skottorando
Scottish *(adj)* Skottorando-no
screw *(n)* neji
screwdriver doraibā
scuba diving skyūba daibing
sculpture *(object)* chōkoku
sea umi
seafood shīfūdo ; kaisan ryōri

sea sickness funayoi
seaside: *at the seaside* umibe de
season *(of year)* kisets
season ticket teiki-jōshaken
seat seki
seat belt shītoberuto
seaweed kaisō
  (edible) nori
second *(adj)* dai ni-no
second class nikyū ; nitō
secretary hisho
security guard kēibi in
seashell kaigara
to see miru
self-catering jisui-no
self-service serufu sābisu
to sell uru
Sellotape® serotēpu ; skochtēpu
to send okuru
to send someone off miokuru
senior citizen kōrēisha
September ku-gats
service *(in restaurant, etc)* sābisu
service charge sābisuryō
set menu teishoku
sex sekks
shampoo shanpū
to share buntan suru ; wakeru
shares *(stocks)* kabu
to shave soru
shaving cream higesori kurīmu
sheet shītsu
shellfish kai-rui
ship fune
shirt shatsu
shock *(electric)* kanden
shock absorber shok abusōbā
shoe kutsu

Slippers

草履

Smoking

喫煙

Soap

石鹸

shoe laces kutsu-himo
shoe polish kutsu-migaki
shop mise
shopping kaimono
  to go shopping kaimono ni iku
shopping trolley shopping kāto
short cut chikamichi
shorts hanzubon
shoulder kata
show *(at theatre, etc)* shō
shower shawā
shrimps ko-ebi
shrine jinja
to shut shimeru
sick *(ill)* byōki-no
  to be sick (vomit) haku
sightseeing kankō
signature shomei ; sain
silk kinu
silver *(n)* gin
  (adj) gin-no
single *(person)* dokshin
  (bed, room) hitori yō no
  (ticket) katamichi
sink *(bathroom etc)* nagashi ; senmendai
sister *(own, younger)* imōto
  (older) ane
  (somebody else's, younger) imōto-san
  (older) onēsan
size ōkisa ; *(clothes)* saizu
skateboard sukētobōdo
skating *(ice)* aisu sukēto
  (roller) rōrā sukēto
to ski skī o suru
ski boots skīgutsu
ski lift skīrifuto
ski pass lifto ken
skirt sukāto
to sleep nemuru

lack of sleep nebusoku
sleeping bag nebukuro
sleeping pill suimin-yaku
slippers surippa
slow osoi
small chīsai
smell *(n)* nioi
to smoke tabako o suu
smoking: *no smoking* kin-en
smoking compartment kitsuensha
sms message keitai meiru
snack karui shokuji
snow *(n)* yuki
  it's snowing yuki ga futteimass
  snowboard(ing) sunōbōdo
soap sekken
soap powder kona sekken
sober *(not drunk)* shirafu-no
sock sokkus ; kutsushta
socket *(electrical)* konsento
soda water tansan sui
soft drink softo dorinku
something nani ka
  shall we eat something? nani ka
  tabemashō ka?
sometimes tokidoki
son *(own)* musuko
  (somebody else's) musuko-san
song uta
soon sugu
sore: *sore head* zutsū
  sore throat nodo no itami
sorry: *I'm sorry* sumimasen
soup sūpu
south minami
South Africa Minami Afrika
South African *(person)* Minami Afrika-jin
souvenir o-miyage ; kinenhin
soy sauce shōyu

Stamps

切手

Station

駅

Stop

止

Storey/floor 階	**spa** onsen
	spanner renchi
	spare parts pāts ; buhin
	spare tyre supeā taiya
	spark plug supāk puragu
	to speak: *do you speak English?* Eigo o hanasemass ka?
	speciality senmon
	speed limit seigen sokudo
	to spell: *how is it spelt?* tsuzuri o oshiete kudasai
	to spend *(money)* (okane o) tsukau
	spicy karai
	spirits *(alcohol)* jōryūshu
	spoon supūn
	sport supōts
Strawberry 苺	**sprain** *(ankle, etc)* nenza
	spring *(season)* haru
	(hot) onsen
	squash *(game, drink)* sukassh
	squid ika
	stadium sutajiam ; kyōgijō
	stamps *(for letters)* kitte
	star *(in sky)* hoshi
	(film) sutā
	station eki
	stationer's bunbōgu-ya
	statue zō
	steak stēki
	steep kyū-na ; kewashī
	stereo stereo
Student 学生	**sterling** igiriss pondo
	sticking plaster bansōkō ; bando eido
	sting *(n)* sashi-kizu
	stomach onaka
	stomachache fukutsū
	storm arashi
	storey kai

175

second storey ni-kai
straight on massugu
strange (odd) hen-na
strawberry sutoroberī ; ichigo
street tōri
street map (residential) jūtaku chizu
  (road) doro chizu
string (for wrapping) himo
stroll: *to go for a stroll* buratsuku
strong (person) tsuyoi
  (material) jōbuna
stuck (jammed) tsumatte iru
student gakusei
stung: *I've been stung* sasaremashta
suburbs kōgai
subway (metro) chikatets
suddenly totsuzen
sugar satō
sugar-free mutō
suit (man's) shinshi yō sūts
  (woman's) fujin yō sūts
suitcase sūtsukēs
summer natsu
sun taiyō
to sunbathe nikkōyoku o suru
sunburn hiyake
Sunday nichi-yōbi
sunglasses sangurass
sunrise hi no de
sunscreen hiyake-dome
sunset hi no iri
sunshade parasoru
sunstroke nisshabyō
suntan lotion hiyake rōshon
supermarket sūpāmāketto ; sūpā
supper (dinner) yūshoku
supplement (n) furoku
surgery (of doctor) shinsatsu-shits

Subway

地下

Summer

夏

Sun

太陽

surname myōji
sweet *(not savoury)* amai
sweetener kanmiryō
sweets ame?
to swim oyogu
swimming pool suimingu pūru
swimsuit mizugi
to switch off suitchi o kiru
to switch on suitchi o ireru
synagogue yudaya-kyōkaidō

T

table tēburu ; tsukue
to take: *how long does it take?*
  dono kurai kakarimass ka?
  take me home ie made okutte kudasai
to talk hanasu
tampon tanpon
tangerines mikan
tap jaguchi
tape *(sticky)* nenchak tēpu
  (audio) kasetto tēpu
to taste *(of something)* ajiwau
to taste *(something)* tabete miru
tax zeikin
tax-free menzei-no
taxi takshī
taxi driver takshī no untenshu
taxi rank takshī noriba
tea *(green)* o-cha
  (black) kōcha
teacher sensei
teenager tīn-ējā
teeth ha
telephone *(n)* denwa
to telephone denwa o kakeru
telephone box denwa boks
to make a telephone call denwa o suru

telephone directory denwa chō
telephone number denwa bangō
television terebi
to tell iu
  (to announce or report) noberu
temperature: *to have a temperature*
  netsu ga aru
temple (o)tera
tennis tenis
tennis court tenis kōto
tennis racket tenis raketto
tent tento
terminal *(airport)* tāminaru
text message keitai meiru
thank you arigatō
  thank you very much (dōmo) arigatō
  gozaimass
that: *that one* (near the listener) sore
  (away from both the listener and speaker)
  see GRAMMAR
the see GRAMMAR
theatre gekijō
thermometer ondokei
thick *(paper, board)* atsui
  (rope, cord) futoi
  (sauce) koi
thief dorobō
thin *(paper, sauce)* usui
  (rope, cord) hosoi
thing mono
  my things watashi no mono
thirsty: *I'm thirsty* nodo ga kawaite
  imass
this: *this one* kore
thread ito
throat nodo
thunder kaminari
thunderstorm raiu
Thursday moku-yōbi

Tea

茶

Teacher

先生

Telephone

電話

Theatre

劇場

Thursday

木曜

Ticket

切符

ticket kippu ; chiketto
  ticket adjustment window norikoshi seisan mado-guchi
  ticket adjustment machine norikoshi seisan-ki
  railway ticket sales office kippu uriba
  ticket office kippu uriba
  ticket vending machine kippu hanbai-ki
tight kitsui
tights taits
time jikan
  this time konkai
  what time is it? nan-ji dess ka?
timetable sukejūru
  (train, etc) jikoku-hyō
tinned kanzume
tinfoil arumi hōiru
tin-opener kankiri
tired: *I'm tired* (watashi wa) tsukarete imass
tissue tisshu
toast tōsto
tobacconist's tabako-ya
today kyō
toilet toire ; benjo
  (polite) o-tearai
toilet paper toiretto pēpā
toiletries keshōhin
toll tsūkōryō
tomato tomato
tomorrow asu
  tomorrow morning ashta no asa
  tomorrow afternoon ashta no gogo
  tomorrow evening ashta no yugata
  tomorrow night ashta no yoru
tonic water tonik uōtā
tonight kon ya
tooth ha
toothache haita

toothbrush haburashi
toothpaste hamigaki
torch kaichū dentō
tough (meat) katai
tour (sightseeing) tsuā
tourist kankō-kyaku
tourist office kankō-annai-sho
tourist ticket kaiyū kippu
towel taoru
town machi
town centre machi no chūshin
town plan toshi-keikaku
tow rope kenin rōpu
toy omocha
tracksuit torēningu uea
tradition dentō
traffic kōtsū
traffic jam kōtsū jūtai
traffic lights shingō
train densha
translation hon'yaku
translator tsūyaku
to travel ryokō o suru
travel agent's ryokō dairiten
traveller's cheque toraberāzu chek
tray (o-)bon
tree ki
trip ryokō
trousers zubon
trout masu
true (real) hontō-no
trunk (luggage) toranku
to try: *can I try it on?* shichaku dekimass
  ka?
Tuesday ka-yōbi
tuna tsuna ; maguro
to turn off (light, etc) kesu
to turn on (light, etc) tsukeru

180

Ticket office

切符売り場

Timetable

時刻表

tweezers pinsetto
twice nikai
twin-bedded room tsuinbeddo no heya
tyre taiya
tyre pressure taiya atsu

U

ulcer kaiyō
umbrella kasa
umpire shinpan-in
uncle (own) oji
  (somebody else's) oji-san
underground (metro) chikatets
underpants (man's) shtagi
to understand: I don't understand
  wakarimasen
  do you understand? wakarimass ka?
underwear shtagi
unemployed mushoku-no
United Kingdom Eikoku ; Igiriss
United States (of America) (Amerika)
  Gasshūkoku ; Beikoku
university daigaku
unleaded petrol muen-gasorin
to unpack (case) ni o hodoku ; ni o toku
unreserved seat jiyū-seki
urgent kinkyū-no
usually futsū wa

V

vacancy (in hotel) akishits
vaccination yobō chūsha
valid (passport, etc) yūkō na
valuables kichōhin
van ban ; wanbox kā
vase tsubo ; kabin
VAT fukakachizei
veal (meat) ko-ushi no niku

181

vegan bejitarian
vegetable yasai
vegetarian bejetarian
vehicle norimono
very taihen ; totemo
video bideo
video camera bideo kamera
video cassette bideo kasetto
video game bideo gaimū
village mura
vinegar su
virus uirus
visa biza
to visit tazuneru
visitor kyaku
  (tourist) kankōkyaku
vitamin bitamin
voltage den-atsu

W

wage chingin ; kyūryo
waist koshi
to wait for... ...o matsu
waiter ueitā
waiting room machiai-shits
waitress uētoress
wake up okiru
Wales Uēruzu
walk: *to go for a walk* sanpo ni iku
wallet saifu
to want hoshī dess
wardrobe yōfuku-dansu
warm atatakai
to wash arau
washing machine sentaku-ki
washing-up liquid ekitai senzai
washing powder kona sekken
wasp suzumebachi

Town

町

Train

列車

Tree

木

watch *(on wrist)* udedokei
to watch TV terebi o miru
water mizu
  hot water oyu
  cold water mizu
waterfall taki
water heater yuwakashiki
watermelon suika
waterproof bōsui-no
water-skiing suijō-skī
way *(manner)* shikata
  (route) hōkō
way in iriguchi
way out deguchi
we watashi-tachi
weak *(physically)* yowai
  (tea, etc) usui
weather tenki
weather forecast tenkiyohō
website uebu saito
wedding kekkon shiki
Wednesday sui-yōbi
week shū
  last week senshū
  next week raishū
  this week konshū
weekday heijits
weekend shūmats
weekly maishū-no
weight omosa
well: *well done* yoku dekimashta
  I am well genki dess
Welsh *(person)* uēruzu-jin
west *(n)* nishi
  (adj) nishi-no
wet nureta
what nani ; nan
  what is it? sore wa nan dess ka?
wheel *(of car)* sharin ; hoīru

wheelchair kuruma-iss
when? itsu?
where? doko?
which: *which is it?* dore dess ka?
whisky uiskī
white *(n)* shiro
  (adj) shiroi
who dare
wholemeal bread komugi haiga iri pan
whose: *whose is it?* dare no dess ka?
why: *why is…?* naze…?
  why did you…? doshte…?
wide hiroi
widow mibōjin
widower otoko-yamome
wife *(own)* tsuma
  (somebody else's) okusan
to win katsu
wind *(air)* kaze
window mado
windscreen fronto garasu
windscreen wipers waipā
windsurfing uindo sāfin
wine wain
  house wine haus wain
  red wine aka wain
  white wine shiro wain
wine list wain risto
winter fuyu
wire *(electric)* kōdo
wireless kōdoress
with *(a person)* …to issho ni
woman onna
wonderful subarashī
wood ki
wood carving *(object)* kibori
wool ke ; ūru
word tango

Vegetable

野菜

Village

村

Wallet

財布